YOUR BEST
Life

How to achieve financial
freedom with the guidance of
a financial adviser

HELEN NAN, CFP®

First published in 2020 by Wealth and Life Planning Pty Ltd
Revised in 2023
www.yourbestlifethebook.com.au
Copyright © 2020 Helen Nan

Author: Helen Nan
Title: *Your Best Life: How to achieve financial freedom with the guidance of a financial adviser*
PRINT ISBN: 9780648770138
EPUB ISBN: 9780648770145
KDP ISBN: 9780648770152

Subjects: Personal Finance, Financial Planning
Book production: www.smartwomenpublish.com
Cover photo: Helen Nan
Original photography: Jason Malouin

What's inside this book?

201 CHAPTER 9: ESTATE PLANNING

Leaving a legacy means not only passing on your assets but also passing down your values and stories to your loved ones. This chapter shows you the different arrangements you need to make to reflect your core values and ensure your final intentions.

211 CHAPTER 10: ADVICE PROCESSES AND THE VALUE OF ADVICE

This chapter explains how you can get the most out of your journey with a trusted adviser, using the adviser's expertise and skills to help you design your dream life. It is difficult to understand the value of advice until you experience it.

225 CHAPTER 11: PLANNING TO LIVE THE DREAM

Financial confusion is one of the most significant blocks to living life on your own terms. This chapter shows you how Richard and Lisa eventually achieve the freedom they crave, as well as the steps to take to design your dream life.

237 EPILOGUE

I explain why I wrote this book and what drives me as an adviser—ensuring my clients' best possible life. I too have the same desire.

Preface

It was 9 May 2011, a rainy day, when I started my new job as a financial adviser at one of Australia's largest financial institutions. I remember seeing the raindrops on the window and feeling thrilled with joy and passion. 'This is life-changing', I told myself—and it was.

I was born in China. My parents are educated professionals, but financial literacy just wasn't part of their curricula. Throughout their working life they acquired liabilities they thought were assets, and constantly struggled on the earning/spending treadmill. Of course, they didn't have any financial plan and spent most of their money on their lifestyle and their children's education. They sent me to finish my studies in Australia, and expected me to study hard, get a degree then a secure job, as most Asian parents hope for their children.

After I moved to Australia, I stayed with my student homestay mum for years. At that time she was in her sixties, and I well remember her financial plan. Every Saturday evening, she poured herself a glass of wine and waited for her Gold Lotto number to be called on TV, dreaming about how she would spend the winnings. She often said, 'If I won a big lotto, I would buy a unit for you in Brisbane'. That never happened, but she won a small prize occasionally, just enough to encourage her to keep buying more tickets.

These are the main money messages I learned from both my Chinese parents and my Aussie mum. When I was studying at university, I read Robert Kiyosaki's book, 'Rich Dad, Poor Dad'. This book opened my eyes to the world of wealth, and I bought his complete series to learn more about money management. Soon after I read those books, I started investing. After a few failed attempts, I realised that reading a few self-help finance books may not be sufficient to make me a successful investor. Hence, I looked for a career in the financial industry.

In 2011, the National Australia Bank wealth consultant program opened the door for my ambition to be realised, and I started my financial planning career at the bank. I had my ups and downs, but I enjoyed my job because I believed that I was improving lives. Since then, I've been growing, not only as a professional but as a person, because of this job.

In 2018, the Royal Commission into Misconduct in the Banking, Superannuation and Financial Services Industry created a perfect storm in the industry, and the profession headed into the next stage of its evolution. The largest wealth companies in Australia shrank and reshaped their advice businesses, and many advisers were seriously considering exit strategies for themselves.

I asked myself many questions at that time too: Where do I stand in my career? What do financial planning clients really want? How can I fulfill my dreams while helping my clients accomplish theirs? Many sleepless nights subsequently ensued. Finally, I left the bank and started my own business at the beginning of 2020 to help my clients on my own terms.

Soon after I started my own financial planning firm, I faced one of the biggest obstacles in my life; one that I never thought to prepare for. No other event in recent history has impacted the whole world as profoundly as the COVID-19 pandemic did. When I navigated my own entrepreneurial journey during the pandemic, I saw some people were able to rely on their own resources to comfortably get by, while others struggled because of their loss of income.

As a consequence, I became even more determined to help empower and educate others with the knowledge and skills that I have learned along the way, as most people, like me, don't grow up with an easy-access 'how-to' money manual.

Money management is confusing; planning your own finances can be hard; and many people don't know where or how to start. I don't want others to make the same mistakes I made in the past as an inexperienced investor, paying a high price for financial ignorance.

In this book, I've incorporated a financial planning framework and strategies into the story of a couple most of us can relate to. Richard and Lisa are both educated, sophisticated, and smart in many aspects of their lives—but not with money.

They are ready to escape a rat-race style of life, and want to seek a life of freedom and abundance. The story tells us how they work with a trusted adviser to design their own future and achieve financial freedom so they can live life on their terms.

Most people don't know what to expect or how to work with financial professionals. This book will offer you guidance and direction by answering these five crucial questions:

What can financial advisers do for me that I can't do for myself? It is often said that doctors make bad patients because they believe they have the knowledge to treat themselves. Like these doctors, do-it-yourself investors or certain professionals who believe they possess extensive experience in investment and finance may think they know better than everyone else. The truth is, we don't know what we don't know.

Where do I start? This is a common question for anyone who wishes to take action and improve their finances. This book introduces you to the process of defining where you are now and what you want in your life, as well as the strategies needed to get there.

When is the right time to see a financial adviser? Now, or before retirement? Most Australians associate financial planning with retirement. However, you can start planning your finances in your 20s, 30s, 40s and 50s, to lead into your early retirement or financial freedom. The earlier you start, the better the outcome.

How do I achieve financial freedom and live the life of my dreams? If you want to be financially free, you must acquire income-producing assets instead of spending all your income on your lifestyle. When passive income from these assets exceeds your expenses, you will no longer rely on your earnings from your job or business, and you will be financially free to live the life of your dreams.

Can I find the balance between money and happiness? Before you decide to make lots of money, you'd better know what brings you true happiness, fulfillment and joy. I call it the meaning of money. When you make money to enhance that meaning, you will maximise the benefits of money and live your life fully and happily.

The financial industry in Australia has been undergoing incredible change and disruption in the last decade. The need for a more client-centric approach to the financial-advice process has been highlighted. Trust is crucial in a long-term relationship in which an adviser asks a family to place their financial future in his or her hands. Clients trust their adviser not because they fully understand what they do, but because they know their adviser understands them.

When clients begin to share their hopes, dreams, and even fears, advisers can help give them a new perspective, turn their desires into numbers and present them with a course of action that inspires them. People working with financial advisers can feel more confident about their future, as there is someone to help them define their goals and dreams, help them avoid costly mistakes, and go through difficult times with them.

Some people may believe that creating a financial plan and seeing it through requires many sacrifices. But, realistically, it's energising and empowering because you are focusing on designing your own future without leaving everything to chance. No matter where you start, you are taking real steps closer to the best life that you desire!

Chapter 1

WHERE HAVE YOU BEEN?

War historians often say that battles are not won and lost in the field, but behind closed doors—in the planning. Life is sometimes like a battle: it has its ups and downs and is directly and indirectly affected by money. Planning your finances becomes inevitable, as it is essentially the planning of a well-lived life. You may ask yourself, 'Am I doing everything I can to get ahead financially?'

Richard found himself asking this question a few times recently. Richard and Lisa were a married couple with two children, aged six and eight. They were in their thirties and had been moving up in their career, buying a home, getting married and growing their family in the last decade. Richard is working as a business development executive at a telecommunication company and Lisa is an education consultant who just transferred from part-time to full-time. They both made a six-figure income and wanted to make the most of their current position—but they did not know where to start. They decided to seek advice.

FIND AN ADVISER WHO HELPS YOU FIND A HOME

The first adviser they met was a middle-aged man from a large financial planning firm. After asking a few questions regarding their reasons for seeking advice, the adviser mentioned the idea of changing Richard and Lisa's super funds to a self-managed super fund (SMSF) and establishing insurances for them. The couple did not make any immediate decisions and wanted to take some time to consider the adviser's suggestions.

On the way home, Richard said to Lisa, 'I don't fully understand the reasons why we should set up an SMSF. He said that he was going to take care of everything, but is it really what we need right now?'

Lisa replied, 'Why don't we seek a second opinion? I don't feel like he fully understands us either, and we haven't thought about our financial goals clearly. I was struggling to tell him what we wanted to achieve at the meeting.'

The couple then sought a second adviser named Mia, who was relatively young and recommended by Lisa's friend, Anna. Mia had many years of experience in both accounting and financial planning. Richard and Lisa received an email from Mia before the meeting:

Dear Richard and Lisa,

Looking forward to catching up. It will be great to meet you and discuss how we can help you map out your future.

'Dreams are the raw material that gets you thinking about what you could achieve.'

What I love most about my role in people's lives is that I am helping them understand and achieve things that they once thought were a pipedream.

The most difficult part of the process is taking the time to figure out what those dreams are. In my experience, I've noticed that when people are put on the spot, they tend to find it hard to pinpoint what they want for their future lives.

I've attached a little template that will hopefully provide some prompts for you and get you thinking about what you want.

If you could fill in some of the questions before our meeting, that would be a great help for our chat.

See you soon.

The email also included the documents that they needed for the meeting, as well as a goals template that they were encouraged to complete before the meeting (which will be explained in Chapter 3).

The adviser explained the agenda for the first meeting: 'I will start by asking you some questions about yourselves, your family, your goals and dreams and your financial experiences. Then, I'll tell you a little about our firm, our philosophy and resources and what potential next steps we want to take from there.'

Drawing from their experience with their previous financial adviser, Richard and Lisa prepared more thoroughly this time—and the meeting went smoothly.

'What is going on in your life, and how do those events make you feel?' Mia asked first.

This question prompted Richard and Lisa to delve into the roots of their financial struggles. Although Richard had earned a six-figure salary, with a generous rise each year, he couldn't seem to save and invest for his and Lisa's future. Lisa had become pregnant soon after she and Richard were married. She had been staying at home as a full-time mum for five years, and the couple relied solely on Richard's income, which was just enough to make ends meet. Lisa took on part-time work three years ago, but the job somehow didn't help with their increased costs of living. After she had received a pay rise, she and Richard both upgraded their cars and planned to move into a larger house that was closer to the school that they wished their children to attend. This would increase their home loan, and the couple realised that it might be too late to start saving or to start considering investments for their future.

The trepidation that they initially felt at the beginning of the meeting quickly disappeared once they began to share their financial concerns and realised that Mia could help them reach their goals. At the end of the meeting, they decided to engage in the financial planning process and take Mia's advice.

UNDERSTAND YOUR MONEY BLUEPRINT

Your money blueprint is your pre-set programming in regard to money. It typically operates outside conscious awareness and drives financial behaviours. The subconscious mind comprises certain ideas and beliefs that are formed primarily in early childhood.

We are programmed in three primary ways around money—by the things we heard, the things saw and the events we experienced when we were young. Ask yourself what your parents taught you about money, as we learn most about this subject at home rather than at school.

'What money messages did you have while you were growing up?' Mia then asked.

To illustrate, she also shared her own story: 'I grew up in a family in which everyone thinks money is not that important. It took me years to change the old habits that had formed from my early childhood—that is, spending most of the money that I made.'

In response, Richard recalled his earliest memory: 'Dad was a sole income earner and had a steady job, but with four children, they were struggling with money all the time. I am a saver, but Lisa likes to spend.'

Richard's dad was a storeman and his mum spent most of her time raising Richard, his two brothers and his sister. His parents were dysfunctional when it came to money. Their financial plan was straightforward: they never set money aside for a rainy day and spent it whenever they had it. They would only save if they needed money for holidays or house renovations, or they would borrow it from the bank. They never owned any investments nor set any money aside for retirement. They spent most of their income on day-to-day living costs and lifestyle. The only financial assets they owned were their superannuation and the equity in their family home.

Richard's mum used to say that 'greedy people are bad people', and his dad's favourite saying was, 'We can't afford it, son. Do you think money grows on trees?' His dad believed that he couldn't make much money due to his low level of education, so he encouraged his son to pursue a higher education.

Richard followed his dad's advice and finished university—but he still struggles with money. If your subconscious mind believes that money is hard to get, then you will encounter problems when acquiring wealth. Your financial success will be limited because you have a poor mindset. The subconscious mind is extremely powerful; it can either help you fulfil your dreams or hold you back from achieving them.

Conversely, Lisa grew up in a middle-class family living on the Gold Coast and enjoyed her childhood by the beach. Lisa's father was away for his work more than he was at home, and she and her older brother were mainly under their mum's care. Lisa's mum groomed her brother to be the centre of attention and told Lisa that she didn't need to worry too much about money, that being a good wife and mother would be enough for her. Lisa had resented her mum for spending all their money on her brother, while Lisa wore the same pair of shoes for the whole summer.

Once she had started to make her own money, Lisa spent most of it on shopping sprees. She is a live-in-the-moment person who tends to spend money for emotional comfort. That new pair of shoes or the latest designer handbag that she has been eyeing can make a bad day turn into the highlight of her week. She is, perhaps unknowingly, compensating for her childhood resentment by spending money on dressing better, driving better and living better than all of her friends from school.

Richard and Lisa had a few arguments regarding her spending habits, but she felt that her husband was micromanaging the family budget and that his attention to their money matters was too obsessive. She had tried to assert her independence in the relationship.

Keeping this background information in mind, Mia continued asking questions: 'Can you rank for me, on a scale of 1 to 10, your level of financial success and satisfaction?'

'I guess we are on about six. We are okay with what we are doing now, but there is room for improvement', Richard answered.

'What strategies do you currently have in place to achieve that improvement?' Mia asked.

With a little chuckle, Richard replied, 'We came to see you'.

'Can you identify what is currently stopping you from achieving that improvement?' Mia continued to ask.

'We find that saving is hard for us. We don't have a lavish lifestyle, but there's always something that needs extra money', Lisa answered.

'It's a lack of knowledge regarding money management. I'm quite ambitious with my career, but money is one thing that I'm always nervous about because we didn't have much when we grew up', Richard told the adviser honestly.

'I can help you with that one. However, you should know that the environment in which you grew up and the way that you think about money shape your approach to spending, saving and investing today. It will affect your financial future if you don't understand and change how you think about money', Mia explained to them.

WHAT IS YOUR MONEY PERSONALITY?

Why can some people with modest incomes build wealth more quickly and easily than others who have a high-paid job, but who are constantly struggling with money? It becomes clear that the amount of money you make is not the main element of financial well-being. Discovering your money blueprint is an essential step in fixing your money problems, because your money blueprint shapes your money personality. There are four general types of money personalities, as detailed below.

Savers

Savers regard money more as a means of obtaining security than of buying desired assets and enjoying life. Savers are not concerned about following the latest trends and derive more satisfaction from observing the balance of their savings account increase than from buying something new. They are conservative by nature and don't take significant risks with their investments.

Some common behaviours for this money personality include:

- They save money for a rainy day and feel nervous if they don't have emergency funds.
- They don't usually spend impulsively and rarely make purchases with credit cards.
- They are always looking for the best deal and take pride in spending less money than someone else for the things they want.

Advice for savers: The problems for savers include excessive wariness and anxiety, which could keep them from enjoying the benefits and sense of security that money can provide. 'Moderation in all things' is good advice for savers. If you are a saver, then you should spend money on something useful and practical to reward yourself. Having a trusted partner or adviser who can provide useful insights regarding this will help you live a balanced life.

The most significant financial rule for savers is that they shouldn't risk the assets that they have worked so hard for. They would do almost anything to avoid debt—and pay it off as quickly as possible if they do find themselves in debt. One downside to this approach can be a lack of action; savers devote substantial time to analysing every potential risk, but then they don't make any decisions at all. It is important to remember that no decision is still a decision, and that opportunities can pass by if they are not seized. Safe savings are indeed better than no savings or bad debt—but they will not increase your wealth. Exploring different investment options and taking calculated risks with a trusted adviser are the keys to your financial success.

Spenders

There are two types of spenders: shoppers and status seekers.

Shoppers often derive great emotional satisfaction from spending money. They cannot resist spending and purchasing items that they do not need. They hunt for bargains and are excited when they find them. However, if shoppers do not address their spending impulses, they could find themselves deep in debt or with crippling credit card bills.

Some of the common behaviours that shoppers exhibit include:

- living in the moment and desiring to make great memories
- only buying new items
- usually being generous and happily treating others.

Status seekers tend to overspend money so that they can raise their social status. They wish to show the world in extravagant ways that they are important and successful, such as by driving expensive cars and living in exclusive neighbourhoods.

The common behaviours of status seekers include the following:

- They think an item is not worth buying if it is not considered the 'best'.
- They retain significant debts to maintain their expensive lifestyles.
- They frequently compare their belongings to those of others.

Advice for spenders: Spenders' problems can be linked to their pretence that they have more money than they do. They are consequently at risk of overspending so they can convince people of their financial success. Therefore, they have relatively lower net worth, even though some of them may make a high income.

A critical step for spenders is to take control of their spending and debt levels, including credit card purchases. They must understand the difference between good and bad debt. Good debt is an investment that will grow in value or that will generate long-term income, whereas bad debt costs money and makes no improvement to one's financial position. Examples of good debts include investment loans for shares and properties, while credit card and car loans are examples of bad debts. The lesson here is that, if you are a spender, you must adopt a lifestyle that is within your means. If you strive for more, acquire it through savings, not debts.

Spending is an act that a person performs to compensate for other areas of his or her life that is found to be lacking. Spenders should thus seriously consider what these areas might be and work to change them. 'Retail therapy' is not a genuine therapy—and it only offers a temporary mood boost. When Richard and Lisa went shopping for their new Audis, they were excited for months in advance, as they did their research, took test drives and weighed the options for styles and colours. The excitement felt from actually purchasing their pristine new cars only lasted for a few months afterwards, as the couple quickly adjusted to their new reality.

To combat spending impulses, ask yourself: what did I buy five years ago that still gives me real happiness and satisfaction? You may not even recall anything. Ask yourself another question: what will provide me with long-lasting happiness and fulfilment? The answers to these questions should include activities that offer the same feelings of accomplishment and self-worth, but without expensive costs.

Avoiders

Avoiders sabotage their financial success because they perceive a negative association between money and being a good person. They are not comfortable with the subject of money due to their lack of interest or understanding. They might not even know how much is in their bank account, and planning for the future is too hard for them. They are thus missing out on certain opportunities that would help them set foundations for a more financially secure future.

Some common behaviours for this type of money personality include:

- believing that rich people are greedy and that money is the root of all evil
- offering numerous excuses to avoid making financial decisions (the less they know about their finances, the better)
- ignoring bank statements and struggling to stick to a budget.

Advice for avoiders: Money avoiders may discard money in an unknowing effort to have as little of it as possible, while simultaneously working excessive hours to make money. Avoiders are thus associated with poor financial health.

If you hate dealing with money, then deal with goals or dreams instead. Your goal could be buying your dream home or studying a master's course. Whatever it is, you should determine how much you need to fund it and then map the plans for achieving it. The desire to achieve a goal is a much more powerful motivator than the desire to avoid something else. When you have a purpose for your money, it will be much easier to find ways of managing it—such as budgeting, bargain hunting and saving—as you have reasons to care.

If you are ready to manage your finances, but ultimately feel frustrated or not motivated enough, then meeting with a financial adviser would be greatly beneficial—he or she can keep you accountable to your commitment for a better and more secure financial future. When you understand that money is a tool for building the life you want and accomplishing what matters to you, you will change your state of mind towards money.

Investors

Investors are always consciously aware of money. They do not make impulsive purchases, like spenders do, because they know that the more money they spend, the less they invest. They also don't just save money, like savers do, as they fully understand their financial situation and try to make their money work for them by taking certain risks.

Some common investor behaviours include:

- They cannot build wealth unless they invest their money.
- They refuse opportunities to spend the money they have today so that they can earn more in the future.

- They expect investments to grow in value or to provide them with a regular income (or both).

Advice for investors: Investors must learn before they can earn. If you are an investor, then every investment that you make in yourself will pay you dividends for a lifetime. In terms of investing, a little knowledge can be a dangerous thing. A 'know-it-all' attitude will not help you achieve anything. If your financial situation isn't turning out exactly the way you want, it means there is something you don't know. Long-term successful investments do not result just from what you know, but also from what you realistically determine that you do not know … and you therefore access help from someone who is an expert in that area. Invest in your financial education and do not hesitate to seek advice when you need it.

* * *

Some of you may find that you have a combination of two or more money personalities. Whatever you find, understanding your money personality is an excellent way to start developing money management strategies that will work best for you.

When you work with a trusted financial adviser to chart your financial journey, they act like a personal trainer and coach. Their goal is to convert spenders and avoiders to savers, then work with you over time and through struggles, so you become an investor with good investment habits.

Most of us are not consciously aware of our behaviours and feelings about money. Like many other parts of our lives, we think that it is just the way we are. Advisers who help their clients understand their money attitudes, habits and dispositions—and who rescript self-limiting money blueprints—can help you grow and protect your wealth more effectively.

YOUR JOURNEY WITH MONEY

Understanding your journey with money is the first step to planning your finance and having the money you need to serve your life. Your journey with money comprises three steps:

- understanding where you have been
- defining where you are now by assessing the resources you have available to accomplish your goals
- discovering where you want to be by identifying your goals, dreams and aspirations.

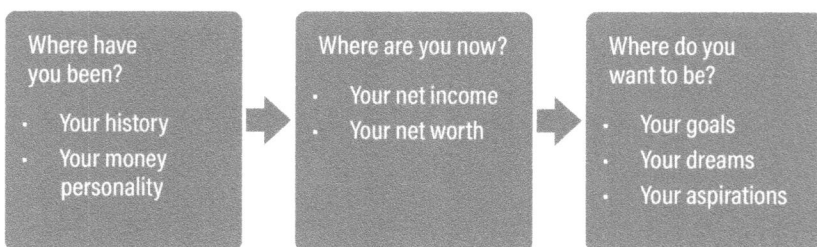

Figure 1. Your Journey with Money

Chapter 2

WHERE ARE YOU NOW?

You cannot make a plan to go somewhere until you know where you are currently. Your financial resources include all your income and assets. They also contain inner resources, such as an ability to earn income, the capacity to save, your core values, and motivation.

'How much are you able to save every month?' Mia asked, back in the meeting.

'We should be able to save every month, but we are currently not doing that', Richard replied.

'How much do you need to live on per month?' Mia continued asking. 'What's the minimum you need to get by?'

Lisa's face went blank as she thought about the answer. 'I don't know', she finally shrugged. 'I've never even thought about figuring it out.'

'We have been discussing doing our budget', Richard added.

'I will give you a piece of advice', Mia began in response. 'You need to know how much you're bringing in, what you have to pay out in necessary bills and how much you can save. Without savings, there can be no investment, and without investment, there can be no growth.'

Every great financial plan begins with a budget, the first step towards making your dreams a reality if you intend to save or invest for your future. A personal or household budget is an itemised summary of expected income and expenses for a defined period, typically one month. You can think of budgets as a tool for achieving your goals and aspirations, as they promote more efficient spending.

'A monthly budget allows you to keep track of your spending patterns and plan for how you will spend and save your money. It is important because the budget relies on balance; if you spend less in one area, then you can save that money for something more important to you in your life. You should provide as much detailed and accurate information as possible to show where your money is coming from and where it is all going each month', Mia further explained.

In response, Richard and Lisa prepared their budget by following these three steps under their adviser's instruction.

1)   Record All Your Sources of Income

As their income is in the form of regular salaries, from which taxes are automatically deducted, Richard and Lisa used the net income amount. Besides their regular salaries, they also receive an accurate depiction of their money by adding in any extra funds that come their way throughout the year (e.g. bonuses, interest and dividends). They should record this total income as a monthly amount.

2)   Create a List of Expenses and Divide Them into Fixed and Variable

Richard and Lisa wrote down all their expenses in a month, including mortgage payments, car payments, insurances, groceries, utilities, entertainment and shopping—basically, they included everything on which they spent their money, then divided the list into two parts: fixed and variable expenses.

Fixed expenses are those that stay relatively the same each month. They include expenses such as mortgage or rent, car payments, insurances, phone bills and electricity.

Variable expenses are the type that may change from month to month and include items such as entertainment, eating out, shopping and holidays. This category is essential as it is where adjustments can be made.

3) Total Your Monthly Income and Monthly Expenses

If you spend more than you earn, then you must make some changes. The results from Richard and Lisa indicate that they have more income than expenses, so they can prioritise this excess and work towards their goals.

When they did this exercise, Richard and Lisa expressed their shock regarding the amount that they had paid in particular categories. 'I don't know we dropped so much cash at restaurants', Richard said.

'I think I should cut back on some of my shopping', Lisa realised, after she discovered that she had spent more than $3,000 on shoes alone in the last 12 months.

The following categories can serve as a guide for anyone who is just starting to plan their budgets (see Table 1).

Table 1. Income & Expenses

INCOME	
Salary/wages (employees)	
Net business income (self-employed)	
Other remuneration (e.g. bonus)	
Interest	
Investment income (rent/dividends)	
Government payments	
Pension/annuity income	
Gifts	
Others	
TOTAL INCOME	

EXPENSES

Rent or mortgage	
Loan repayments (e.g. personal loans and car loans)	
Grocery	
Dine out	
Utilities	
Insurances (e.g. home, car, health, life, income protection and others)	
Clothing and clothing care	
Auto expenses (e.g. petrol, services, registration, repairs and car wash)	
Medical and dental expenses	
Transportation	
Childcare	
Education	
Hobbies	
Entertainment	
Vacations	
Charitable donation	
Others	
TOTAL EXPENSES	

NET SAVINGS (INCOME LESS EXPENSES)

This exercise underscores your ability (or inability) to save money. The net savings amount illustrates where you financially stand—the larger the number, the more you have to work with towards realising your goals. If you have little or no savings at all, then you are on an earning–spending treadmill, running faster and faster towards a financial vision that will not come any closer. A sudden change in your circumstances, such as a loss of income or the realisation that retirement is near, can be an effective wake-up call that often accompanies feelings of regret for missed opportunities.

Based on their budget, Richard and Lisa should be able to save more than 25 per cent of their income; however, they have saved nothing in the last 12 months. There always seemed to be something that drastically reduced their savings, even if it was small: a surprise bill for car repairs or a moment of weakness when their favourite brand had a large sale. The couple feels like they are working hard, but they never seem to get anywhere.

'People say that they will invest when they have extra money one day, but that day never comes along. When you have difficulties in saving, paying yourself first is the way to go', Mia explained.

'Pay yourself first?' Lisa repeated, raising her eyebrows.

'Every payday, the first thing you do when the money hits your transaction account is transfer a percentage into three key accounts: emergency fund, investment fund and superannuation. If you use this process, you won't need to worry about holding money aside for a savings plan. You can spend the rest of the money after you have paid the accounts first', Mia said. An illustration of Mia's suggestion can be observed in Figure 2.

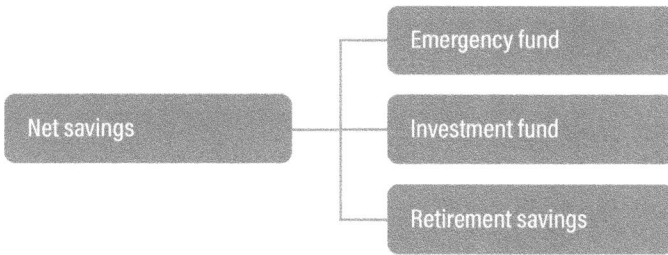

Figure 2. Distribution of Net Savings

Your net savings should be paid into three categories:

- The 'emergency fund' is intended for unexpected expenses, such as unemployment or health emergencies. Advisers usually recommend three to six months of living expenses.
- The 'investment' is your money-making machine which produces passive income. Building a money-making machine is a key to your financial success as the more assets you accumulate in your money-making machine, the less you rely on your paying job.
- 'Retirement savings' mainly indicate your superannuation which pays you an income at retirement.

Many people underestimate their expenses when they do their budgets. When you calculate your expenses, you should also account for any unexpected bills, such as unplanned car repairs. A good rule of thumb is to pay an extra 10–15 per cent. Richard and Lisa began automating payments of 15 per cent of their income into these three categories, which was calculated based on their primary goals.

'The second step is to notice where you have money left over or where you can cut back so that you have money to dedicate to your goals. Variable expenses are the first areas to consider for spending cuts', Mia further instructed.

Richard and Lisa began to dine out less often, and Lisa assigned a limit regarding how much she would spend on shopping every month for her family and herself. If you are doing this part of the budget yourself, you should evaluate your spending on needs once you have adjusted your spending on wants. An example would be internet expenses: you may need the internet at home, but do you need the fastest internet package available?

'If there is still a gap between your goals and your saving capacity, you can consider adjusting your fixed expenses. This will be much more difficult, and it will require greater discipline. For example, your health insurance—if you haven't done so for many years, then you may need to review your policy. Negotiating your home loan interest rate with your bank or refinancing every few years can also help you save interest, as lenders might offer different rates to new customers that don't always match what existing customers are paying. Ensure that you carefully weigh your options', Mia said.

'Try not to spend rises or windfalls', she further added. 'If your salary increases or you receive a bonus, instead of living it up with any extra money that comes in, add it to your investments. A small amount of savings per month can significantly influence your net worth over time due to the effect of compounding.'

'The last point, but not the least: simply creating a budget will not solve your financial problems. You have to stick to it. It's important to regularly review your budget to ensure that you are on track. After the first month, take your time to compare your actual expenses against what you had forecast in the budget. Then you will know where you have done well and where you still need to improve', Mia concluded.

Most people regard financial planning as being primarily concerned with investments. However, financial planning is based on a budget and driven by goals. You cannot control the external environment (e.g. investment market), but one thing you can control is your spending habit. Richard and Lisa started saving 15 per cent of their income in different accounts and gradually increased the percentage once they felt comfortable enough to do so. Working through a budget increases your awareness of the categories in which you could reduce spending as a means of increasing your savings and investments for your main goals and dreams.

Struggling to follow a budget and savings plan signifies that the two do not align with your true values. You must tie your money to what matters most. Prioritising how you use your money may entail giving up on certain purchases you might usually make, such as a lavish lifestyle or expensive holidays. However, if you reduce your spending, you will become instantly wealthier and have more choices. Conversely, if you increase your spending, you will automatically become poorer and have fewer options. Essentially, you sacrifice what you want in the short term for what is more important in the long term.

Changing your spending habits may take time, but it is eventually rewarding, and you will be one step closer to your ideal life.

THE DIFFERENCE BETWEEN INCOME AND NET WORTH

'I felt like we were never getting ahead. We worked hard and secured well-paying jobs, and up until recently, I realised that we were not accumulating any assets. We are paying into the home loan, which reduces very slowly, and we have saved very little and made no investments', Richard mentioned in the meeting. However, he had also told his adviser that he and Lisa were considering upgrading their house after Lisa went back to full-time work. The larger house in the better neighbourhood that they were considering may double their home loan amount.

In regard to building wealth, how substantial your income is does not really matter. Yes, you can more quickly increase your wealth with a larger income, but more income also creates new temptations and complexities; it does not guarantee that you will more quickly increase your wealth or have a large nest egg when you retire. Your income is like water flowing through a hose; the higher your income, the larger the flow of water. However, wealth is like a bucket that you are trying to fill with water. If you have a high-flow hose but your bucket has a large hole in it, you will never fill that bucket as quickly as you want. Your entire financial security depends on your net worth, and passive income from assets will offer you more freedom to achieve your dreams.

Net worth is simply the amount by which assets exceed liabilities. It is a concept that can be applied to individuals and it serves as a benchmark for measuring financial health. Let's take a look at Richard's and Lisa's net worth in Table 2.

Table 2. Net Worth

ASSETS	LIABILITIES
Family home: $900,000	Home loan: $650,000
Home content: $20,000	Car loans (2): $95,000
Motor vehicles (2): $130,000	Credit cards: $8,000
Superannuation:	
Richard—$185,000	
Lisa—$70,000	
Savings: $5,000	
TOTAL ASSETS: $1,310,000	**TOTAL LIABILITIES: $753,000**

NET WORTH (TOTAL ASSETS – TOTAL LIABILITIES): $557,000

Their net worth is positive, but it is mainly composed of their superannuation and home equity. Almost half of their net worth lies with their superannuation—which they cannot currently access—and their recently purchased two Audis will depreciate quickly. They don't have any investment assets which produce passive income, and this is not aligned with the personal direction they desire to take.

Surprisingly, many high-income earners have low net worth and live pay to pay. Richard described himself as a saver: he does not spend much money on clothes and shoes like Lisa does, but he does spend his money on something else—looking successful by driving a fancy car and planning to move into an exclusive neighbourhood.

He came from humble beginnings, managed to finish university despite his background, and climbed the corporate ladder. He lives and operates in a culture that is driven by high incomes. Richard feels that appearing successful is an implied require-ment for continuing to build his high-income career. He is not alone in this belief: we are trained to measure ourselves by our possessions, and we shop for items that enhance our self-image or social status to reflect our standards of success.

People who work in large law firms, accounting firms and investment banks are required to move in circles around other people who are much wealthier. They drive expensive cars, wear costly suits and live in the exclusive neighbourhoods where their customers live. The biggest problem with keeping up with Joneses is that people tend to compare themselves to the wrong Joneses.

The medical field is an excellent example of high-income careers—and many doctors are struggling to pay back large debts, as they tend to buy expensive houses too early in their careers. Doctors who spend many years in medical school tend to amass debts and have expensive lifestyles because financial literacy just isn't a part of most medical curricula, despite the high level of education. The doctors' problem is not how they make money, but how they manage it.

When our income increases, our lifestyle does as well. Lifestyle inflation affects us all. When we make more money, we start spending that extra income on expensive holidays and on acquiring large debts. High-income earners generally become more concerned with freeing their time; they wish to spend more money on factors of convenience, such as dining out frequently, which replaces the tradition of home-cooking meals.

LIVING YOUR DREAM LIFE NOW OR LATER

There is a fine line between saving and living. If you make too many sacrifices now to save for the future, you might be left with feelings of dissatisfaction and unfulfillment, which only become stronger with time.

Living the dream means that you should enjoy both your present and your future. However, if you spend all the money you make today and do not save or invest for the future, then you will not enjoy a fruitful outcome. Are you currently using your money to enjoy your now, or are you saving it for your future? An adept adviser will help you choose a balance. If you haven't yet ascertained what the exact balance is, you will find your answer as you go through the process of identifying what you value most in your life in Chapter 3.

Those who have been on the income fast-track during their careers might feel excessive optimism and believe that they will make more income in the future. However, in reality, no one is irreplaceable. People should prepare for the day when their income will no longer be there, either due to their employer's decision or their own choice to walk in a different direction. There is nothing wrong with Richard and Lisa's current home, which they built themselves. However, the higher income raised the bar in their lives because they now believe that they can afford a more expensive house and cars. They thus begin to justify the reasons why these items are necessary.

Mia offered further insights on this topic: 'If you purchased that $1.5 million house that you inspected last week, your home loan would be doubled and you would use most of your current net savings on increased loan repayments. This means that you must sacrifice the other priorities that you mentioned before so that you can have an expensive house. You have two options: spending your money by living in the present, even if it means incurring larger debts, or working towards your goals and freedom, which are more important to you. One way generally leads to debt, while the other generally leads to prosperity. It's your life, so it's your choice.'

Chapter 3

WHAT DO YOU WANT IN YOUR LIFE?

If you want to live the life you desire, then you must possess a clear vision of what that life will look like. The process of uncovering where you have been previously, where you are today and where you are headed is essential for your financial planning process; your money has a purpose and your life will unfold alongside that purpose in the future. If you want to have the best life possible with the money that you have, then you must understand that purpose.

Unfortunately, most people would rather spend more time on planning their annual holidays than on discovering what exactly they want in their lives and the specific steps required for achieving that. Without planning reasonable steps and making the effort to achieve them, everything that you desire remains only a hope.

Like other couples their age, Richard and Lisa desired to pay off their debts, fund their children's education and pay for their family vacations.

Richard told Mia at the first meeting that his long-term goal was to retire in 20 years. 'I am 38 now. It would be ideal if I could retire at age 58.'

Mia responded with a question: 'Why do you want to retire at age 58? Have you ever visualised your ideal life when you retire?'

'I've never thought that far, but I don't want to wait for government pension age and rely on Centrelink'. After a short silence, he added: 'I don't want to be at home and watch TV all day when I retire; I may still work. I want to be financially ready so that I can have my own options'.

'Would you like to have the freedom to choose what you do at the age of 58?' Mia asked.

'Yes, that is exactly what I want', Richard responded. He gradually revealed what had happened to his dad and how it had affected Richard. His father has been working all his life, but when he was close to his retirement age, he did not have enough retirement savings for his wife and himself. He was still working in a job that he did not like at the age of 63 and he needed to work a few more years to receive a government

Age Pension. Richard did not want to be in the same position as his dad.

'On a scale of 1 to 10, how important is achieving financial freedom at the age 58 for you?' the adviser further asked.

'It is a long-term goal, I know, but it is very important for me, so maybe eight', Richard answered.

'How will you feel if you achieve this goal, and how will you feel if you can't achieve it?' Mia asked.

Richard thought about it. 'If I achieve my financial freedom at age 58, I would be very confident about every money decision that I made. If I can't achieve it, then I have to think about alternatives—either to work longer or reduce my living expenses at retirement, which will be very disappointing. I will feel that things are not under control', he answered.

* * *

I have found that people desire a trusted adviser to help them clearly define what they want in life and to offer them guidance and direction in achieving it. Many people are not able to verbalise what they wish to accomplish when an adviser simply asks, 'What are your goals?'

Financial planning is helpful for people at all stages of their lives, not only for those in a particular age group or income bracket, because taking control of your financial life requires careful planning. If you compare financial planning to taking a long trip, you realise that you will need a map to help you arrive at your destination. Financial planning provides you with that road map, which outlines where you want to go and the goals that are your destinations along the way.

There are a few steps to setting financial goals so that you can reach your destination:

- Start by identifying what you want in your life.
- Identify your core values.
- Identify and prioritise your goals.
- Determine your emotional connection to your goals.
- Understand the significant motivations that underlie your goals.

WHAT DO YOU REALLY WANT?

When people are about to set their goals, the first challenge they encounter is their inability to express what they wish to achieve. Richard does not have a clear picture of what he wants, though he knows what he does not want (living like his parents). Once you realise and face what you do not want, the next step is to discover what you do want in your life. If you intend to uncover the life that you wish to live, ask yourself three questions that George D Kinder posed in his book, *Lighting the Torch*:

- 'Imagine that you have all the money you will ever need: how will you live your life? Would you change anything?'

- 'You visit your doctor who tells you that you have five to 10 years left to live. The good part is that you won't ever feel sick. What will you do in the time you have remaining to live? Will you live your life differently?'

- 'This time, your doctor shocks you with the news that you have only one day left to live. Ask yourself: What dreams will be left unfulfilled? Is there anything you missed in your life?'

Let's look at these questions more closely.

If you had all the money you need: The first question is powerful because many people place unnecessary constraints on their ability to reach their goals. We are so afraid of not having enough money for the things we want that we do not dare to even dream for more. We are also afraid of verbalising what we want, in case others won't accept us. The result is that we hide our dreams and aspirations behind the mask of conformity and people-pleasing. Asking ourselves what we really want offers us the opportunity to dream. If we want to uncover what is truly important to our lives, we must first remove any artificial constraints that limit our ability to dream.

'If I have enough money and time, I would like to take my children on a world trip. Those kinds of memories will stay with them for the rest of their lives', Richard said.

If you had five to 10 years left to live: Many of us know people who have come close to death, then completely changed their lives: they suddenly thought about their existence in a different way and re-evaluated their priorities as a result. We all know that we will die one day, but we do not know when. We also imagine that we have plenty of time to do what we desire and we waste our time on activities and items that do not add much value to our lives.

'If we will only live 10 more years, today is more important than ever. We must discover what our ideal life looks like now so that we can make a plan to pursue it today', Richard stated.

'If I only have five to 10 years left to live, I would want to have my own business. It would also provide me with the flexibility to spend more time with my children. How many soccer games have I missed with my children since I went back to work? They grow up very fast', responded Lisa.

Most of us have experienced unfulfilled dreams or we have missed aspirations as time has gone by. However, we still have the opportunity to live our lives differently—so we can fix it now. We do not need to wait for someone to present us with a death sentence in order to have a real appreciation of the value of our lives.

If you had one day left to live: As you might imagine, this is the most emotionally challenging question. It often reveals what you find most important and how you want to be remembered, which can be determined by the way you choose to live. It is only by imagining your non-existence that you can sense what is most important about your existence.

'If today is your last day, what have you left unfinished? It's time to stop making excuses for why you aren't doing that right now. Start working towards that today', Mia instructed.

Most of us set our goals too low—we strive to achieve little and settle for small dreams or no dreams at all—despite having extraordinary talents and potential. We tend to reside in quiet desperation in the wake of our unrealised dreams and feel that life slips away through our fingers. Asking ourselves those three George Kinder questions can help us identify what is important in our lives, and it can help us design our lives around those answers.

IDENTIFY YOUR CORE VALUES

Core values are a person's fundamental beliefs and reflect his or her sense of right and wrong. We experience fulfilment when we consistently honour our core values. However, when we don't honour our values, we are likely to escape into a bad habit and feel frustrated. There are different methods for discovering our core values, but this book mainly considers our core values in relation to money.

The best financial plan in the world will be useless if you do not follow it and take the necessary actions. The most significant reason we fail to implement financial plans is that we forget our motivations. Goals themselves are not motivations; you must know the reasons behind your goals. The 'why' underlying your goals are your core values, the intangibles that make the pursuit of those goals genuinely meaningful to you; and goals are the tangible results that you seek.

How can you find out your core value? Bill Bachrach explains this well in his book, 'Value-Based Selling'. Ask yourself a simple question: What do you find important about money? Perhaps it is security or success. Perhaps it is something else entirely. Whatever it is, write it down. There is no right or wrong answer, as everyone is different. You can then ask yourself: what is important about that answer to you? Write your response down above your first answer. You can then ask yourself again: what is important about that response to you? Repeat the process as many times as you need to until you reach your final answer—which is the most important reason for you. Richard and Lisa have done this exercise with the adviser, and their answers from the bottom to the top of the value staircase are as shown in Figure 3.

Richard

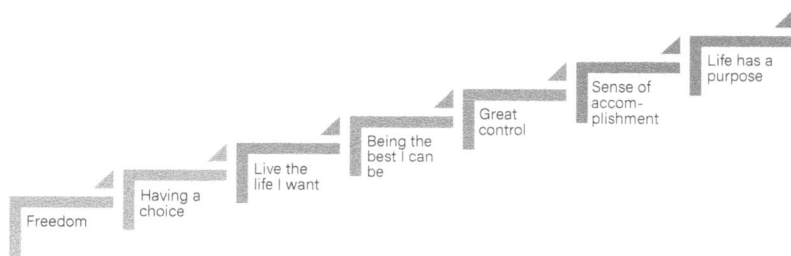

Lisa

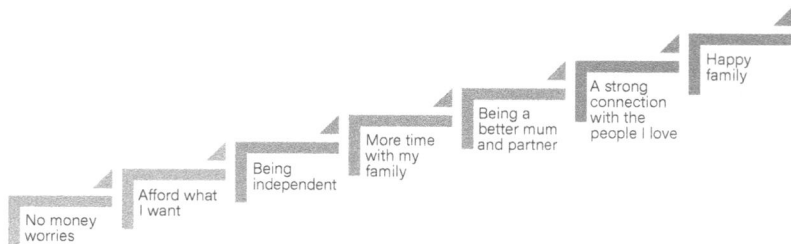

Figure 3. The Value Staircase

The most meaningful value for Richard is to live a life with purpose. For Lisa, it is a happy family. The lesson from this exercise is that you should pay attention to whether you currently reflect your values in your daily life. If you experience much dissatisfaction with your life, then you may not be living in alignment with your values—you may need to re-evaluate what is most important to you. A feeling of satisfaction with life is what results when a person's course of action is in harmony with his or her inner desires and values. Once you have established your core values, the goal-setting process will be easier to complete.

YOUR GOALS MUST BE CLEARLY DEFINED

Goals drive financial planning and connect our outer life to our souls. They present our dreams in practical dollar terms, and those dreams infuse financial planning with energy and direction.

Have you ever believed that the goals you set are far from your reach, or that you find yourself always procrastinating? If so, you should set your goals in a more constructive way—in a 'SMARTER' way.

A 'SMARTER' goal signifies one that is specific, measurable, achievable, realistic, time bound, exciting and risky. For example, your goal might be to save $150 per week over the next 12 months for a holiday to Las Vegas that you have always dreamed of.

In keeping with the SMARTER mindset, the goal should be:

- **specific**—you should know exactly what you wish to achieve
- **measurable**—you should decide how much you need to save or invest to achieve your goals
- **achievable**—you should assess the possibilities of what you could achieve or what you could do
- **relevant**—you should ensure that your goals are aligned with your core values and that you understand how you will achieve them
- **time bound**—you should determine when you want to achieve your goals
- **exciting**—you should feel inspired by your goal and it should lift you out of your comfort zone into your desire zone
- **risky**—you should stretch your abilities to reach your goal, as the uncertainty regarding whether you can actually reach your goal challenges you.

In addition to this, you should be aware that personal financial goals will differ in the length of time that is required to achieve them. For example:

- Short-term goals span from one to three years.
- Medium-term goals span from three to five years.
- Long-term goals span from five to 10 years.
- Lifetime goals span indefinitely.

With this knowledge in mind, Richard and Lisa set their own goals with different timeframes, with Mia's assistance:

- short-term goals—paying off all bad debts such as credit card and car loans of $103,000 in the next three years
- medium-term goals—Lisa owning a business in five years, with estimated set-up costs of $80,000
- long-term goals—having a world trip with their two children, with estimated costs of $60,000 and funding their children's university education, with estimated costs of $70,000 in 10 years
- lifetime goals—achieving financial freedom in 20 years, with an annual passive income of $100,000 (in today's dollars).

After we understand our goals, we must then prioritise them. When prioritising goals with clients, advisers should address the three main elements of an investment decision: time horizon, rate of return and risk profile. In general terms, the longer the timeframe of your goals, the higher the anticipated rate of return on investment and the higher the degree of volatility (which will be discussed in more detail in Chapter 5).

What emotions will you experience once you have achieved your goals? Richard's long-term goal is to take his family on a world trip, the reason for which is linked to his history. When he was in high school, Richard's school organised a trip to Tasmania—but he did not attend because he wanted to save $1,000. A thousand dollars may have been substantial savings at the time, but Richard realises now that he can never travel back in time to enjoy those memories with his friends. He believes that he will feel a sense of accomplishment and joy when he can provide this experience for his children, and he will have a happier and more connected family through the trip. A valuable lesson can be learned here: when we have an emotional connection with a goal—not just a mental and physical one—we become committed.

When the reason for your goal is extensive enough, you will do whatever is required to achieve it. However, if you do not have a strong reason, then any excuse can stop you or tempt you to procrastinate. Lisa revealed that she wants to own a business in five years. When she returned to full-time work, she realised that she missed spending time with her children. Conversely, she also wants to be financially independent so that she can afford whatever she desires. She believes that she can obtain both these desires once she owns a successful small business.

It is important to note that you should revisit your goals and adjust them when needed, and then celebrate when you achieve them. Table 3 outlines a grid of categories that can help you more easily identify your goals.

Table 3. Life Goals Template

CATEGORIES	GOALS	PRIORITY	TIMEFRAME	TOTAL COST
Financial				
Family				
Work/Career				
Personal growth				
Leisure/ Adventure				
Fitness				
Community				
Charitable				
Legacy				

Note: Priority code 1 = very important, 2 = important, 3 = moderately important and 4 = it would be nice, but not necessary

FINANCIAL FREEDOM

In a normal lifecycle, people accumulate wealth until retirement, then begin to consume what they have acquired after they retire. However, in the lifecycle of financial freedom, instead of eating into your funds after retirement, you build an investment portfolio generating passive income exceeding your expenses, and you continue to grow your wealth in perpetuity.

Richard had asked Mia at a goal-setting meeting, 'How much will be enough for us to have financial freedom?'

'For your situation, financial freedom means having enough passive income from investments so you can afford the lifestyle you want for your family, without relying on your income from employment. Realistically, the number you should aim for is 25 times your annual expenses. If you need to spend $100,000 per annum, you will need $2.5 million', she had answered.

In theory, you need to have saved at least 25 times your annual expenses to be financially free after retirement.

For example, if you spend $100,000 per annum, you will need 2.5M ($100,000 x 25). Assuming your investment grows by 5 per cent (adjusted for inflation) over a year, you now have $2,625,000 invested. Imagine you'll be withdrawing at the rate of 4 per cent a year (2.5M x 0.04 = $100,000).

The value of your investment would look like this a year after withdrawal: $2,625,000 – $ 100,000 = $2,525,000. Your investment will have grown by $25,000 after withdrawal.

The key is to never touch your investment principal, and only withdraw less than your investment growth. However, the length of time an investment portfolio will last is based on a few variables that we'll discuss here.

Asset allocation: This is the percentage of growth assets (shares and properties) versus defensive assets (fixed interest and cash) that determines the level of risk/return in the portfolio.

The higher the percentage of growth assets, the greater the returns will be over the long term, but the more volatile your investment will be in the short term.

Tax: Tax is something we can't ignore when it comes to investing. If you pay income tax on that $100,000, the net income after tax will be much less. Minimizing your tax on your investment in the tax-advantaged structure is vital for smart investors.

Inflation: Inflation is one of an investor's worst enemies. At 3 per cent inflation, a dollar is worth about 74 cents in 10 years; 55 cents in 20 years; and 41 cents in 30 years. Once you stop working, you start to pay more attention to inflation and spending power. Hence, your long-term investment returns need to be greater than inflation and withdrawal needs combined.

Withdrawal rate: If you withdraw both investment gains and principal, you might run out of money before you run out of life. Imagine you retire at the age of forty, and need your money to last another 50 years. Hence, when the investment market is down, you might consider using an emergency fund or starting a side hustle so you withdraw as little as possible from your long-term investments.

Living expenses: The amount of money you need to live on today and in the future is based on the lifestyle you want to live. Coming up with an exact figure for future expenses is unrealistic. You might also have once-off large expenses at different stages of your life, such as buying a new car or funding your child's college education.

The path to financial freedom can be unpredictable and complex. We will discuss more in detail in our later chapters.

FINANCIAL PLANNING STAGES

Financial planning is similar to building a home. You are the architects of your dream home and you have the picture of the final product in your mind. However, when we discuss the topic of financial planning, most people spend too much time concentrating on only one aspect of financial planning—wealth accumulation. We try to invest our time and energy into identifying investments that can generate high returns. As such, we may ask ourselves whether investment planning alone is sufficient for planning our future. To answer this question, we must first consider financial planning in four distinct stages: wealth protection, wealth accumulation, wealth preservation and wealth distribution (see Figure 4).

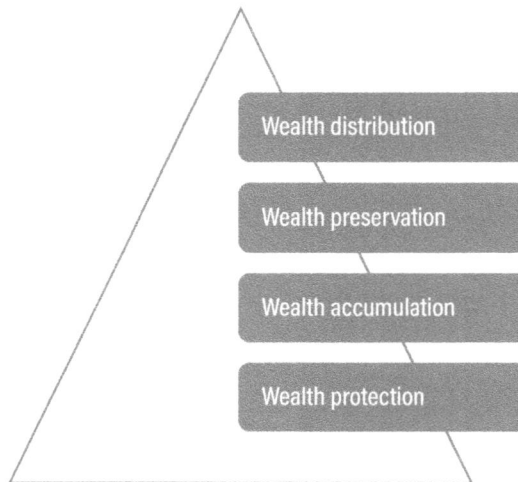

Figure 4. The Four Financial Planning Stages

Wealth protection: Would you drive your car without any insurance? Of course not. Would you plan your future without insuring your most valuable asset (income)? The answer should be the same. If financial planning is similar to building a dream home, then wealth protection can be considered the foundation of the home. A sound financial plan that is designed to build and preserve wealth is not as valuable if it does not provide financial protection in the event that your income ceases. Protecting your current and future earnings from the effects of a long-term illness, disability or even death must be considered in equal measure with wealth accumulation.

Wealth accumulation: The process of building your dream home is exciting and empowering, but the focus then shifts towards saving money and building wealth. Investing that is done correctly is both an art and a science. It is an art because people are emotional beings, and our decisions are affected by our values, past experiences, greed and fears. Investing is also a science, as it involves money making that requires strategies and formulae. A person must balance both art and science to become a successful investor.

Wealth preservation: After your dream home has been built, maintenance becomes the key to keeping it alive. People approaching retirement should consider methods for preserving their wealth through effective planning. The wealth preservation stage involves taking time to evaluate the investments that provide you with ongoing, stable income streams at retirement, as well as those that minimise the effects of the volatile market, so that you can ensure that your money lasts.

Wealth distribution: You have worked diligently to build your dream home, and now it is time to create an effective wealth distribution strategy for passing your nest egg to your heirs. Estate planning addresses how income or wealth will be distributed to your heirs to ensure that you and your family can maintain the lifestyle that you have worked so hard to establish.

* * *

Capitalising on certain opportunities for protecting, growing, preserving and transferring your wealth requires the sophisticated guidance of a professional who knows and understands your needs. A great financial plan typically addresses the right balance of everything, so that you can face your future with confidence.

Chapter 4

HOW TO PROTECT
YOUR WEALTH

When Richard came home from his work one day, Lisa sensed that something was wrong. When she asked him, he told her that he had met his high school friend, Julia, who was going through a difficult time in her life.

Julia's husband, Ian, had passed away from a heart attack four years ago and had left her with three children, aged five, eight and 12. They had two mortgages of $420,000 and $350,000 against their family home and an investment property, respectively. They had purchased their investment property at the height of the property 'bubble' in a mining area, but it had declined in value from $350,000 to $150,000 since its purchase. The rental income she was receiving only covered half of the loan's interest expenses. Julia could not afford to pay both mortgage repayments, as she worked as a part-time administrator in a publishing company. Ian had been working as a self-employed plumber for an extensive time, but he never organised his superannuation or his life insurance policy. His parents and grandparents have all exhibited great longevity in their lives, without any health problems, so he never felt the need to organise personal insurance for himself.

The bank eventually foreclosed on the two mortgages, and Julia and her children had to move into her parents' home. There was still an $80,000 debt that remained after she had sold the two properties. To try to pay off the debt, Julia decided to sell her possessions. She sold Ian's car for $10,000, as well as his business equipment. She also sold most of her furniture to her friends and family, as many of the items could not fit in her parents' house and she could not afford the $30-per-week rate for storage.

She was extremely busy because she worked now at a super-market, loading the shelves at night, in addition to her day job. She was also working hard to repay the $50,000 that remained from what she and Ian had borrowed from their previous mortgages. Her parents helped her look after her children, who were not happy, as they rarely saw their mum after their dad passed away.

Keenly feeling for Julia and the situation she was in, Richard said to Lisa: 'When we see our adviser for our review meeting this time, we need to review our insurance policies and top up some of them if necessary'.

ARE AUSTRALIANS DANGEROUSLY UNDERINSURED?

There is a serious issue with Australians being underinsured, as many do not have insurance policies that will enable them to meet their financial obligations and help them maintain their lifestyles if the worst were to happen.

According to estimates from Rice Warner's report on under-insurance in Australia, only a third of the working population has income protection insurance. Worryingly, 55 per cent of Australians would not have enough money to last three months if they had no occupation.

Of the total number of working Australians, 94 per cent are likely to have some life cover, with an average cover amount of approximately $344,500. However, this figure can be misleading, as it is skewed by a relatively small proportion of the population (typically those with relatively high incomes and active financial advisers) that has a high level of cover. For this reason, the median cover level is estimated to be approximately $143,500, which is more appropriate when measuring the insurance cover that is held across Australia. It is only twice the median household income.

The proportion of the working population with total and permanent disability (TPD) insurance is slightly less than that with life insurance, at 81 per cent. This is because super-annuation funds may only offer a default life insurance cover to some of their members. However, the average and median cover amounts are only $237,000 and $99,5000, respectively.

You may think, 'It won't happen to me'. We certainly hope that it won't, but statistics show that men have a 1 in 3 chance of suffering from cancer and that women have a 1 in 4 chance of developing cancer before the age of 75, with an average of 131 deaths every day. With such harsh statistics for cancer alone, it is clear that insurance should not be considered lightly—because when you feel that you need insurance, it may be too late.

WHY DO WE NEED INSURANCE?

When Mia mentioned 'risk management strategy' to Richard and Lisa when they met, Richard was not convinced of the concept of having adequate personal protection.

He told Mia, 'Well, I have some cover in my superannuation. My parents are in good health—even my grandparents are still alive. Insurance is not a priority for me at this stage, and I would like to direct that money to building wealth for our future'.

Mia thought about how she could best explain her point to her clients. She stated, 'I know that you built your current home'.

'We built it 10 years ago, the year we were married', Richard replied.

'What was the most exciting part of the whole process?' Mia asked.

'That was our dream home, after we built it', Richard answered.

'If you built the house without appropriate foundations, how long do you think it would last?' she asked further.

'It might not last very long', Richard admitted.

'I can understand that the most exciting parts of your financial plan are the investment strategies that are designed to increase your wealth and help you achieve your dreams, aspirations and goals. But, what is the one thing that you need every month to ensure that you continue to implement and complete your investment strategies?' Mia asked.

'That would be my income', Richard replied, suddenly realising what Mia was trying to explain to them.

'You are absolutely right! So, how long would all your investment strategies last if you suddenly had no income at all?' she asked.

'Not long', Richard responded, understanding. 'They may have to stop immediately'.

'Protecting your income is not the most motivating part of your plan, just as laying down the foundations wasn't the most exciting part of building your dream home. However, they are both necessary processes for building your wealth and your home. So, would you agree that securing your income on an ongoing basis should become part of your wealth-building strategies?' Mia asked, taking her time to explain her point clearly.

'Yes, we would. I never thought about it that way before', Richard replied, as he and Lisa both nodded in agreement.

Protecting your wealth will not be the most exciting part of your financial plan. Even some advisers prefer to overlook this part of the process. All investment strategies that are designed to accumulate wealth are based on the presumption that income is received on an ongoing basis. As such, how can you justify creating a sound financial plan before protecting and securing your ongoing income in the first place?

The answer is that the better prepared you are to meet financial challenges, the more efficiently you will recover financially and emotionally. There are a few steps that you must take to protect yourself and your family from unexpected risks:

- Assess what cover you need.
- Determine how much you need for each policy.
- Find a high-quality product that is based on afford-ability and the sustainability of the cover.
- Review your policies regularly.

SELF-ASSESSMENT CHECKLIST

This checklist will help you quickly assess your current level of financial protection, as well as determine the steps you will need to take to upgrade your financial security.

Table 4. Self-Assessment Checklist

TOOL	DESCRIPTION	HAVE	NOT SURE/ REVIEW	DON'T HAVE
Emergency fund	Money that is set aside for unexpected situations. You have enough to cover unexpected repairs, urgent travel or loss of income in your savings.			
Life insurance	A product that pays out a sum of money to your family/beneficiaries in the event of your death, or if you are diagnosed with a terminal illness.			
TPD insurance	Insurance that pays out benefits if you are unable/unlikely to work on your own or in any occupation for which you are suited by training, education or experience.			
Income protection (IP)	Replaces your income if you cannot work due to sickness or injury, as well as pays a monthly taxable benefit.			
Trauma insurance	Provides a lump sum of money to cover immediate medical expenses and other financial needs when a critical illness or injury occurs.			
General insurances	Includes car, home and content, and landlord insurances.			
Private health insurance	Insurance that can help pay for the cost of your treatment as a private hospital patient, or for out-of-hospital health care services.			

HOW MUCH DO YOU NEED?

Going through the process of determining your insurance needs with a trusted adviser is an important step for ensuring that your personal insurance is done right. People struggle to objectively and thoroughly identify their lifestyle income needs in 'what if' scenarios; having a trusted adviser will help you make the right choices regarding the types of insurance and levels of cover.

'How much is your worth for your family in terms of income?' Mia asked Richard.

'My income is $150,000 per annum', Richard replied.

'In the event of your unexpected death, what would you like to replace?' she asked.

'I'm not sure. Maybe 100 per cent of my income. What do you suggest?' Richard asked the adviser.

Mia thought about her reply. 'Realistically, your family wouldn't actually need $150,000 per annum, since they spend less when you're not around. They might only need about $120,000 per annum. But we must also consider some other factors. Do you think that you will still be earning $150,000 per annum if you were still around in 10 or 20 years?' Mia asked.

'I think I will be making more than that with pay rises', Richard answered.

'I think that too. We must also consider another factor—inflation', Mia began explaining. She considered the factual information that would help Richard and Lisa easily understand this part of insurance. 'Your living costs will increase as inflation reduces the purchasing power over time. The average inflation rate has been between 2 and 3 per cent in the last few decades in Australia. Accounting for your possible pay rise and inflation, if you passed away, then the amount of benefit that your family requires can replace your current income of $150,000 per annum, assuming that they are conservatively receiving 5 per cent returns every year. Your family may need less than $150,000 per annum in the early years, but we will have a buffer to reinvest the amount that they do not need for increasing living costs and other future commitments. Would you feel comfortable with that?' she asked.

'Yes, I would', Richard replied.

Every adviser may have a different method for organising insurance, which requires an analysis with their clients. This is based on the family's income needs in the event of a death. Mia had gone through a set of questions with both Richard and Lisa regarding their lifestyles and income needs in the event of either of their deaths, temporary or permanent disabilities, and critical illnesses and injuries.

FIND A HIGH-QUALITY PRODUCT

Finding a high-quality product that matches your individual insurance needs and that rests within an affordable budget is the next step to obtaining the best value from your insurance.

Advisers should assess your whole financial position and recommend the policies that you can keep for the long term. Affordability, sustainability and claim ability are the goals when you are in the process of choosing your insurance.

'You need to go through an underwriting process when you apply for insurance', Mia explained.

'Underwriting process?' Richard asked, confused by the term.

'Yes. Have you ever bet on a horse race?' the adviser asked in response.

'A few times, but not too often', said Richard.

'Insurance is much like a betting system. If you were to put a large bet on a horse, you would research its form and pedigree thoroughly. In a one-million-dollar personal insurance policy, the insurance company assesses their risk of losing that money, should a claim be made. In order to assess that risk, the applicant must disclose all of their medical history, as well as any other factors that may affect the level of risk, such as exposure to dangerous pastimes and other family medical histories. The insurer may even require more certainty of someone's health risk via medical tests, if they feel they need it', Mia carefully explained.

'So, they are going to collect information on all our medical histories, pastimes and family histories when we apply for insurance, as well as assess the risks?' Lisa summarised.

'Yes. The insurance company looks carefully at their own exposure to risk factors in their policies, and researching your form is called "underwriting". Fortunately, when they accept your application, you are locked in: this happens only once, so they will be very thorough to begin with.'

Buying insurance entails transferring your risks to an insurance company. Insurance underwriters evaluate the risks and exposures of potential clients. They decide how much coverage the client should receive, how much they should pay for it, or whether the insurance company should even accept the risk of insuring the client. Once they approve the application, the insurance policies become legal contracts—'non-cancellable' or 'guaranteed renewable' contracts with terms that cannot be altered. After the insurance policy is enacted, the policy cannot be cancelled, nor can renewal be rejected, as long as you pay the premium.

The certainty of protection that the client has in place will not be jeopardised for non-cancellable or guaranteed policies:

Change in health: The insurer cannot have the terms of the insurance altered if the clients develop illnesses once the policy is enacted.

Change in occupation: Once the policy is accepted, a change in profession (e.g. to a higher-risk occupation) cannot result in a change of premium.

Change in smoker status: A previously declared non-smoker who takes up smoking cannot have their premium increased.

Change in pastimes: Performing a 'hazardous' activity that was not planned at the time of application cannot have the terms of the policies altered.

Multiple claims of Income Protection (IP): After an IP is claimed, the insured party can make further claims if necessary, and the premium cannot be increased.

It may take one to three hours of your time to have this level of certainty during the application process. In relation to direct life insurance that is bought online or default insurances that are included in your superannuation without any underwriting, insurers are taking a greater risk. They thus limit their risks to only conditions or events that occur after the policy commences, and they uncover pre-existing conditions at the claim time instead of assessing a client's risk when he or she applies for the insurance. We buy insurance products that we hope we'll never need, but the claims are the 'moment of truth' in any insurance products. The easier it is to take out insurance policies, the more difficult your claim will be. As a consumer, you must ensure that you pay to claim the benefits when you need money most. Fully underwritten insurance policies will offer you a high level of certainty.

REVIEW YOUR POLICY

Insurance is not something that you can 'set and forget'. Regular policy reviews that a trusted adviser performs can determine whether the policy is still suitable according to your needs and whether it still meets your financial goals. Knowing when to review your insurance products is as important as choosing the right policies. Certain considerations to keep in mind when doing this include:

- **Changes to your income**—If your income increased, then you must ensure that your benefits are sufficient to cover your increased lifestyle costs in a 'what if' situation. When you are close to your retirement and cut back on some hours, you may need to consider reducing your level of cover.
- **Changes in family situation**—If you are married or have a newborn baby, you must ensure that your loved one is covered and update your beneficiaries accordingly. If your children become independent and move out of your home, then you may need less cover.
- **Changes in health and lifestyle**—If you quit smoking, you must update your policies, as there is a significant difference regarding the premiums between smokers and non-smokers. If your policy has loadings and exclusions and your health has improved since you took out the policy, then you must ask to review your policy with an underwriter.
- **Changes in your financial situation**—If you obtain a new mortgage or pay off the existing mortgage, you may need to consider increasing or reducing your benefits in relation to your debt levels accordingly.
- **Changes in employer and work**—If you change your occupation, especially to a lower risk role, you must review your policy, as IP and TPD insurance premiums can be different, based on the level of associated risk.

It is essential to understand that there is no such thing as the 'best' life insurance company and policy. The best for you does not necessarily have to be the highest-rated product or the cheapest product; it just has to have the features and benefits that apply to your situation and needs.

INSURANCE MISCONCEPTIONS

Ensure that your priorities are assigned correctly. Most people have insurance for their homes and motor vehicles, but they fail to insure their most valuable assets—their lives and their abilities to earn income over the long term. You must not think that you don't need personal insurance if you don't have children or a mortgage. There are insurances, such as IP, TPD and trauma insurance, that you should consider much sooner in life, such as when you secure a full-time job. You are your own greatest asset.

Insurance replaces what you currently have, and you should not make a profit from replacing your loss. As mentioned at the start of this chapter, underinsurance is a problem in Australia, though overprotection is a waste of your money.

You only need to insure something that you cannot replace. Why do you have insurance for your mobile phone, but you don't protect your income? An excellent general rule that can be followed is to insure adequately against losses that you cannot replace and to self-insure small losses and pay them out of your pocket.

Lots of working people with superannuation have some insurance cover in their super fund. How likely is it that a default life or TPD policy through super is a good match for your needs? The 'one-size-fits-all' mentality rarely delivers the best insurance solution.

THE IMPORTANCE OF INCOME IN FINANCIAL PLANNING

The key to achieving your goals and living your dream life is providing and maximising one factor in your life—your income. There are three specific situations in which your adviser would maximise you and your family's income—during your working life, after your working life and for the dependents, if you die early:

1) Income during your working life

- Employment or business income
- Passive income from investments
- Income replacement of 70 per cent IP, plus 30 per cent trauma insurance.

When you have a job, you make your money from employment. When you have your own business, you earn your money from the profit of the business. If you wish to stop working, then you would need passive income that can fully cover your expenses, which we call 'financial freedom'. I will thoroughly discuss how to create your passive income in the next two chapters.

However, if you must stop working due to a disability and you must replace your income, income protection insurance will be critical. The problem with IP insurance is that it only covers 70 per cent of your pre-disability income, as claimants must be motivated to return to work once on claim. If you would like to have a 100 per cent income replacement, you can fill the 30 per cent gap with trauma insurance benefits, which pay a tax-free lump sum for any critical illness, or severe injuries in some situations. Most IPs in the market do not cover involuntary unemployment, so you must have enough emergency funds to secure yourself if job security is a concern. Ask yourself what type of income replacement you have in place now. If you have none, then it is time to consider having some.

2) Income after your working life

- Superannuation plus Age Pension or additional investment income streams.

When you retire, your employment or business income ceases. In Australia, primary income sources during retirement are derived from superannuation, Age Pension and other investment incomes.

For some people, insurance through super is the only way it can be affordable, as clients have debts to repay and other household bills to manage. However, you will have less money earning compounding returns for your retirement, which will later influence your cash flow during retirement. Making salary sacrifices into your super fund to cover your insurance premium is one method of reducing this influence, if you have a sufficient cash flow.

3) Income for dependents if you die prematurely

- Life insurance.

If you pass away prematurely, then you will require either life insurance or substantial assets that can generate sufficient income for your dependents. The life insurance benefits that you require will depend on the percentage of income that your dependants need per annum, as well as the number of years that it is needed, which depends on your dependents' ages and your surviving partner's earning capacity.

* * *

In terms of a sound investment process, the ultimate value that an adviser adds is the ability to minimise both the desire to sell his or her client's investment down-market and the need to sell by reducing the risks from death, disability and loss of employment. If you developed a sound investment strategy, but failed to support it with adequate insurance covers, then it would collapse at the first claim event. It may jeopardise all your savings or result in additional debts that would take you years to repay. Protecting your wealth is as important as building your wealth, and it should be part of your wealth accumulation strategies.

Chapter 5

HOW TO BUILD WEALTH

I wish I could show you how to turn $10,000 into a million-dollar investment in a few years, or build a business venture and become a millionaire in five years. This book is not about that as those scenarios don't apply to most people. But I will show you the strategies that average people can apply so they accumulate a million-dollar portfolio.

Successful money management requires 70 per cent discipline and 30 per cent skills. I will teach you the strategies and the skills you need to master to become a successful investor. You can then apply those skills, combined with good habits, to turn your dreams into reality.

'You said we needed 2.5M to achieve our financial freedom. How can we achieve that? There are too many options and I don't know where to start. Do I need to open a share trading account or buy an investment property?' These were some of Richard's questions at the meeting.

'If you want to be financially free, you must acquire income-producing assets instead of spending all your income on your lifestyle. I call this your money-making machine. When passive income from a money-making machine exceeds your expenses, you will no longer rely on a pay cheque from your job', Mia responded.

Building a money-making machine is the key to your financial success. The more assets you accumulate in your money-making machine, the less you rely on your paying job. We all want to have the freedom to explore the world and live life on our own terms. Every dollar you invest in a money-making machine helps you take one step closer to your financial freedom.

When we consider investment options, we are generally aiming for two factors—growing the value of your investment, and also generating income for both the present and the future.

There are four traditional asset classes that you can consider: cash, fixed interest (FI), shares, and property. An asset class is just a type of investment. Defensive assets such as cash and FI generally have a lower risk and a lower return potential. Conversely, growth assets such as shares and property have higher risk and higher return potential. (see Figure 5).

Shares and property are the assets that have positive returns after inflation and taxes. In the current high inflation environment, cash in the bank cannot keep up with inflation and decreases in value every day. Savers will eventually become losers if they do not invest in growth assets.

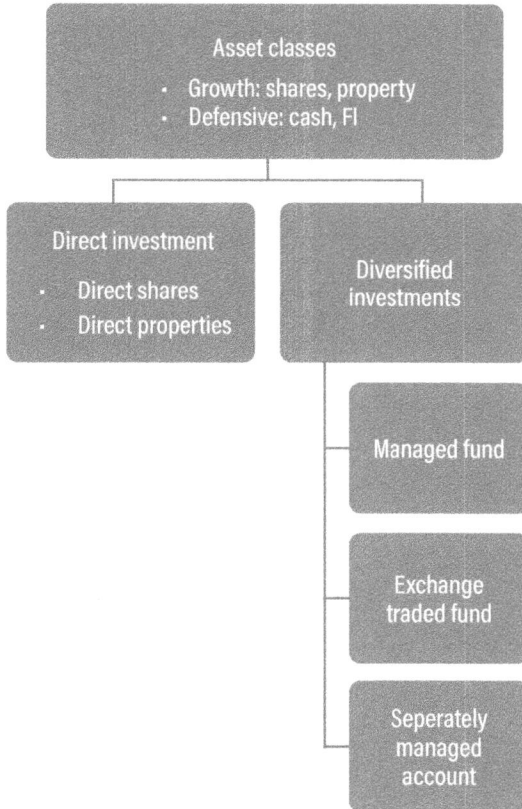

Figure 5. Investments Overview

SHARES

'Is it the right time to buy shares?' Richard asked, to which Lisa added, 'Isn't that too risky?'

'The right time to buy shares is now, so long as you have the money. The right time to sell them is never, unless you need the money; and the great risk is in not owning them. The real risk comes from people not knowing what they are investing in', Mia explained.

'The share market has made millions of people rich, and it has been one of the best places for the long-term investor to build wealth', she further explained. Mia asked, 'Do you know why?'

'If you buy an iPhone, then you are a consumer of the Apple company. But if you own Apple shares, then you are the owner of the business. Stocks present ownership of the business; bonds lend money to businesses and real estate houses that business. Neither bond nor real estate can provide ownership in the economy's ability to produce that shares do', Mia answered.

Boxing Day Share Sale and Diversification

'I hear that some people lose lots of money from the share market. Why is that?' Lisa asked in concern.

'Shares have a good record of return in the long term, but the share market is volatile in the short term. How people react in a volatile market will decide how much money they ultimately receive. Investing in the share market is not a numbers game, it is a mind game. When the share market rises, you might hear from your friends and family about how well their shares are doing and how much money they are making. You hesitate at first, but then you might eventually buy shares yourself. Soon after, the share prices may begin to drop. When the prices fall below what you paid for them, and you realise that you are losing part of your original investment, you may feel an edge of panic set in. If the market continues to fall, you will probably feel even more anxious. When the market drops to a total of 35–40 per cent, it's likely you will not be able to hold on anymore. You will abandon your goals of financial freedom or your dream retirement and you will sell the shares. However, the market will surely start to rise again and you will be standing on the sidelines, realising that the opportunity you might have had will be forever lost. This is how people lose their money during a bad market', Mia explained in detail.

'If you invest in shares, you must know that the share market does not always rise. You should expect one losing year in every four or five. When do you normally do your big shopping?' When Mia asked this question, Richard looked at Lisa and teased, 'This is the question for you, I guess'.

'Normally, I do my shopping when there is a big sale, like on Boxing Day', Lisa answered, a little confused.

Mia smiled. 'Investment is the same. It involves buying shares when they are on sale. It is the perfect timing now for you to buy instead of sell.' Mia continued: 'Most people sell when share prices drop, and you buy them when they are cheap. I call it the Boxing Day share sale. It is how wealth is transferred', she explained. Richard and Lisa looked at each other and nodded.

'Now, we know that we must hold onto our shares or even buy-in when the market falls. However, if the company in which we invest goes bust, then we will eventually lose all our investments, right?' Lisa asked, drawing attention to this concern.

'This is an excellent point', Mia nodded in agreement. 'You can break a pencil, but you cannot break 50 pencils tied together. That's diversification. For new and inexperienced investors like you, a diversified share portfolio is the way to go.' She further added: 'You can diversify across time, not only across different shares'.

'Across time? What does that mean?' Richard asked in confusion.

'We call it dollar–cost averaging. You keep adding money to your investment every fortnight or month; you are then reducing the risks and increasing the returns over time. It can make the dumbest person in the world wealthy', Mia explained with a grin (see Table 5).

She continued with her explanation: 'You invest $1,000 in a share each month when the market price fell from $20 and then recovered to $20. The shares were purchased at an average cost of $15.06 ($5,000/332). After five months, the investment was valued at $6,640 (i.e. 332 shares at $20 per share), and you made a profit of $1,640 ($6,640–$5,000). If the shares had been purchased at the commencement of the five months with $20, you would not have made any profit when the shares returned to their purchase price at the end of the five-month period'.

Table 5. Dollar-cost Averaging

MONTH	AMOUNT INVESTED	SHARE PRICE	UNITS PURCHASED
1	$1,000	$20	50
2	$1,000	$15	66
3	$1,000	$10	100
4	$1,000	$15	66
5	$1,000	$20	50
TOTAL	$5,000		332

'I guess it is an easy way to invest in the share market. You will never know whether the market will go up or down tomorrow', Richard agreed.

'You are absolutely right! You can completely ignore timing in the market with dollar–cost averaging. This is also an ideal strategy for someone with a regular income, but who doesn't have large sums to invest', Mia said.

Table 6 below highlights the characteristics of cash, FI, share and properties. Defensive assets such as cash and FI focus on income and growth assets such as shares, while property focuses on both capital growth and income.

Table 6. Cash, FI, Share and Properties Characteristics

ASSET CLASS	CHARACTERISTICS	RISK	POTEN-TIAL RETURN
CASH Includes bank deposit, term deposit, savings and cheque accounts, and cash management	It's stable. You probably will not lose money, but you probably will not gain much either	Low	Low
FI Fixed-interest securities, such as bonds, pay a fixed-dollar income in the form of a coupon payment for an agreed period of time. Bonds can be domestic and international.	Receiving a moderate return in exchange for a moderate amount of risk, as well as receiving a stream of income and offsetting the risk of share investments. **Main risks:** Bond prices and interest rates move in the opposite direction. Therefore, rising interest rates could push bond prices down. The bond's issuer may stop making promised payments, or be unable to repay the principal.	Low or moderate	Moderate

ASSET CLASS	CHARACTERISTICS	RISK	POTEN-TIAL RETURN
SHARES Represents partial ownership of a company, which enables the investor to share in the profits of future growth. Shares can be domestic or international.	Receiving a larger return in exchange for more significant volatility. **Main risks**: The value of shares tends to fluctuate more than that of other assets for numerous reasons, including poor performance of certain companies and concern for the economy. The minimum suggested timeframe is 5–7 years.	High	High
PROPERTY Generally involves buying a property directly or investing in property securities.	Having a higher risk than FI, but less risk than shares. **Main risks for direct property:** Less liquid than other asset classes, resulting in a higher recommended minimum timeframe. Entry and exit costs are significantly higher. Minimum suggested timeframe: 7+ years	Moderate or high	Moderate or high

We build our wealth from growth assets, which are shares and property. Understanding what to expect from each asset class will inform you in making appropriate investment decisions that are based on your individual varying needs and timeframes.

MANAGED INVESTMENTS

The easiest way to access diversified investments is investing through a managed fund, an exchange traded fund (ETF) and a separately managed account (SMA). Table 7 illustrates a summary of the differences for these three common diversified investments.

Table 7. Differences between Managed Funds, ETFs and SMAs

MANAGED FUND	ETF	SMA
Pooled with other investors and invest according to the fund's objectives	Pooled with other investors, buy and sell on the Australian Securities Exchange (ASX), like shares	Customised managed accounts personally tailored to your needs
Small-amount initial investment	Small-amount initial investment	Some managed accounts require a larger initial investment, but have more transparency with investments and more effectively manage your tax liabilities
Passive and active management style; return on the active management style depends on the abilities of the manager	Passive and active management style, but passive style is a popular strategy. Passive management style cannot outperform the index, and there is a brokerage fee every time you buy and sell units	Active management style, and returns depend on the manager's abilities

Managed Funds

A managed fund pools your money with funds from other investors, which an investment manager uses to trade shares or other assets for you. There are two main types of managed funds:

- **Passive funds:** These typically have lower fees and seek to match their holdings to an index—a measurement of a particular financial sector. They are suitable for investors who seek index-like returns and lower management fees.
- **Active funds:** Fund managers for this type of fund play a more decisive role; they pick and choose certain investments to outperform the market. Actively managed funds usually attract higher fees and create more short-term realised capital gains from a higher portfolio turnover.

The choice between active or passive management will depend on how efficient the markets are and the client's goals. Active management will be difficult, in terms of continually adding value in a truly efficient market. However, if clients have specific goals to achieve or need to protect their investments in a down market, then the active management style can play a more significant role. For retired clients who care mostly about income, a dividend growth that is focused on actively managed funds will be more beneficial. Many advisers use a combination of both to further diversify their portfolios and help manage overall risks.

ETFs

ETFs are a pooled investment option that can be traded on the share market. Like a managed fund, ETFs allow consumers to invest in a basket of assets or companies that have a single trade. While managed funds will perform transactions once a day, ETFs are traded constantly, with prices available in real time.

There are active and passive ETFs and the passive manage-ment style is a popular strategy for ETF investors. Due to the straightforward way that investment decisions are made, ETFs will typically have lower management fees than managed funds, but passive ETFs cannot t outperform the market.

Young investors who have minimal savings to invest can have a diversified portfolio with relatively low fees and investment thresholds if they choose ETF.

SMAs

Managed accounts are experiencing a rapid rise in popularity in recent years. An SMA is a portfolio that is built for an investor, and invests in a variety of assets or asset classes.

SMAs can be tailored to your preferences and personal needs. Due to this personal approach, a managed account may likely require a higher initial investment, and it is suitable for someone who has a large capital to start with. You retain direct ownership of your investment and you could manage your tax liabilities more effectively than with other investment vehicles.

DIRECT INVESTMENTS AND MANAGED INVESTMENTS

'Why do you want to invest?' Mia asked.

'Well, I've changed my job from part-time to full-time recently. It was a means for us to have some spare cash every month and I do not want to waste it. We want our money to work for us. We want to have enough money to afford family holidays and our children's education, as well as enough to help our children buy their first homes', Lisa answered.

'For me, it is more about freedom, choices and doing what we love. We are making a good income for our age, but I do not feel that we are making any progress with our finances', Richard responded, raised his concerns. 'I do not know much about investment, but I do not mind taking some risks—I mean, taking calculated risks.'

'You mentioned share trading and buying investment properties. They are direct investments that require much expertise and attention. Would you like to spend extensive time analysing the market and company financial statements and managing your investments?' Mia asked.

'I want to know how to plan our financial future, but I am not prepared to spend much of my time being a financial expert. That is why we came to see you—we wanted advice from an expert', Richard explained.

If you want your assets to be managed by a professional, there is a cost—there are fees that you must pay to the fund manager. Directly owning assets such as property and shares can be time consuming. You do not need much specialised knowledge to invest in direct property, but it is more complicated in terms of managing it. Studying numbers and analysing statistics should be a vital part of a client's due diligence before he or she invests in the share market. Numerous share investors are overwhelmed by all the information that is available, and by the volume of research that is required. If you have the time and interest to manage your own investments, then doing so yourself can provide you with great control over your assets.

In contrast to long-term investing, traders choose to take a much shorter-term perspective on a company's share price and they aim to acquire profits from short-term price movements in the share market. Traders buy shares to sell and investors buy shares to hold, though trading shares may certainly seem more exciting than a long-term investment. If your goal is to make money in the short term, then trading shares can be very profitable. However, trading is accompanied by higher risks in and outside the market, and you, as the client, will be saddled with fees and taxes that persistently chip away at your returns. You will also potentially miss out on the potential gains that long-term investors enjoy, but with much less effort. Many people who set out to trade shares fail, mainly because they are undercapitalised or because they cannot control their emotions during the short-term movements in the market. Being a successful trader requires significant education and experience, as well as more substantial amounts of available money. Trading is thus not for everyone. Investing your money for the long term is a much smarter and less stressful method of building one's wealth. However, when investors sell shares in a down-market, they become traders and subsequently lose their money.

Managed investments are a suitable option for clients who do not have the time or the expertise to directly invest in shares and property, as well as those who simply do not want to be hassled by the day-to-day effort of owning shares and properties. Clients who choose managed investments prefer to outsource their investment decisions to someone else so that they can spend their time on what they enjoy.

CRYPTOCURRENCY

'I invested a few thousand dollars in cryptocurrency a couple of years ago when it was at the peak, but it's almost worth nothing now. I've heard some people made a fortune from crypto. Is it something I should invest in more?' Richard asked.

'Shares represent ownership in companies, and property is a tangible asset you can see and touch. They both have capital growth and generate income. However, crypto lacks intrinsic value and doesn't generate passive income. It is a very high-risk investment and you need to be prepared to lose everything you put in,' Mia explained.

Cryptocurrencies are a new paradigm for money, and a large sum of people's wealth has been transferred into the market. It was first developed as a digital currency that allows people to make payments directly to each other through an online system.

Cryptocurrencies are decentralized networks based on block-chain technology, allowing them to exist outside the control of governments and central authorities. It allows easy and fast money transfers and is almost impossible to counterfeit or double-spend. However, cryptocurrencies are not legal tender in Australia and not widely accepted as payment.

Cryptocurrency became popular among investors as we often heard that someone created substantial fortunes by investing in the early stages of its development. But it is a high-risk investment and very volatile.

There are a number of cryptocurrencies, and Bitcoin is the most widely traded and well-known of them. It was made available to the public in 2009 and is basically worth nothing. It increased from $1 at the beginning of 2010 to almost US$70,000 toward the end of 2021, before falling to around US$35,000 in early 2022. It dropped further to less than US$20,000 in early 2023. Cryptocurrencies have no legislated or intrinsic value, and the price of crypto can fluctuate at an extreme level often based on what people want to pay for them in the market.

What factors can influence the price of crypto? Normally media hype, public announcements, and social media posts by individuals with large amounts of cryptocurrency. In the wake of Bitcoin's success, some are willing to take the risk of buying other early-stage coins, some of which may easily go bust in a few years.

Apart from the volatility of a crypto investment, there are other risk factors you need to be aware of before you invest your money. Many cryptos are not commonly considered to be financial assets, and the platform where you buy and sell crypto may not be regulated by ASIC. If your account is hacked and stolen, or your investment is switched off by the token developer, you have little hope of getting it back.

Before you invest any money in crypto, ask yourself: 'How much can I afford to lose?' If someone has a low risk tolerance level or is close to retirement, I recommend they have less than 5 per cent of their portfolio invested in crypto, as it will become very volatile with a higher portion.

Like other investments, if you fully understand the risks of cryptocurrency, and your risk profile is high enough to accept it, you can include it in your diversified portfolio as it has a low correlation with the stock and property market.

You can also buy shares in a company with crypto interests, such as Tesla, PayPal, Square and Bitfarms. If you invest in diversified managed funds, index funds, or exchange-traded funds, you might already have some exposure to cryptocurrency, as the companies with crypto interests might be included in the funds.

THE INVESTMENT PROCESS

| Resources
Risk profile
Time horizon | INVESTMENT ALLOCATED:

Very conservative
Cautious
Moderate
Balanced
Aggressive
Very aggressive | TAX-EFFECTIVE STRATEGY

RISK MANAGEMENT STRATEGIES:

Start early
Diversification
Dollar-cost averaging
Boxing Day sale | GOALS

Short-term
Mid-term
Long-term |

Figure 6. Investment Process

Once you know what you want in your life, the next step is to determine what you can use to help you achieve your objectives. Your resources are not merely indicating your net savings and net worth in dollar terms, they also illustrate your strengths and weaknesses in regard to money that can be used for effective planning. The investment you choose will significantly depend on your risk tolerance level and goal timeframes.

'Should we invest all our money in the share market?' asked Richard.

'No', Mia replied simply. 'Shares are volatile and you must invest in the long term to see those good returns. It is money intended for your future and it should not be used now', she added.

'For our short or medium-term goals, where do we need to invest our money?' Lisa asked.

'We first need to test your risk profile and then get into asset allocation to balance your investment with cash, FI, shares and property', Mia answered.

YOUR RISK PROFILE

'Everyone is different when it comes to investing. Some people are natural risk takers and feel comfortable with higher-risk investments. However, some people are more conservative and cannot stand the thought of losing money. Others desire high returns, but they do not want to take any risks at all. If you remove the risks, then you will also remove any opportunities in the investment world. You can't avoid the risk, but it can be managed. Your next step is understanding your risk profile and discovering what types of investors you are', Mia explained.

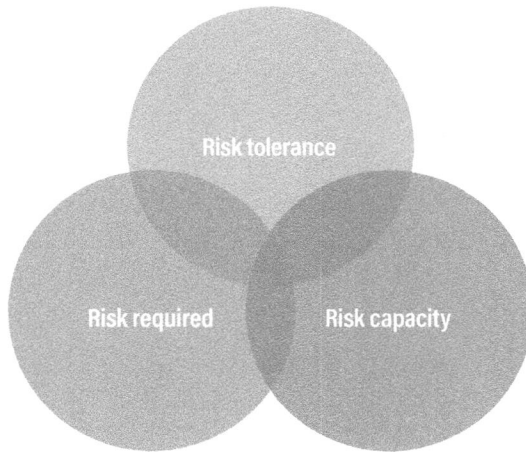

Figure 7. Risk Profile

Risk profiling is a process intended to discover the optimal level of investment risk that you can take. It does so by balancing your required risk, risk capacity and individual risk tolerance. Financial advisers normally guide their clients through the questionnaires to assess their risk profile:

- **Risk capacity** is the maximum level of financial risk that you can afford to take.
- **Risk required** is the optimal level of risk that you need to take.
- **Risk tolerance** is the level of financial risk that you want to take.

There is often a mismatch between these three categories of risk. If your goals require that you take a high level of risk that you cannot tolerate, then you may need to compromise your goals and reduce your needs. It will be your decision regarding whether you should stay out of your comfort zone and take more risks or whether you should adjust your objectives to match your comfort level.

It is difficult to assign a dollar value to the concept of peace of mind. If the volatility of your investment causes you to lose sleep, then that could be a clear cue for you to adjust your asset allocation. After all, we save and invest to improve our quality of life—not to develop ulcers!

Consequently, Richard has exhibited a very aggressive risk profile, while Lisa has exhibited a more balanced one. How much risk you can afford to take depends on the timeframe of each goal and your risk profile. Growth assets such as shares and property are not suitable for short timeframes, as their values fluctuate. However, if you save for your retirement in 20 years, then you have time to ride out the ups and downs in the investment markets—and you can take a higher level of risk.

ASSET ALLOCATION

'What is asset allocation?' Lisa asked.

'Let me ask you a question: why did you buy the Audi?' Mia responded with another question.

'Because it has its unique appeal, it is comfortable and it is reliable on the road', Lisa answered.

'If I gave you a blank check to buy five vehicles, would you buy five of the same car?' Mia asked.

'Of course not. I would buy five different cars', Lisa replied.

'I would like to recommend that you buy a Ferrari for aggressive driving, a Mercedes for moderately aggressive driving, a Volvo for conservative driving, an SUV for all weather conditions, a Jeep for the really bad driving conditions and your own Audi for stable and balanced driving', Mia recommended.

'How is that relevant to asset allocation with our investment?' Richard asked.

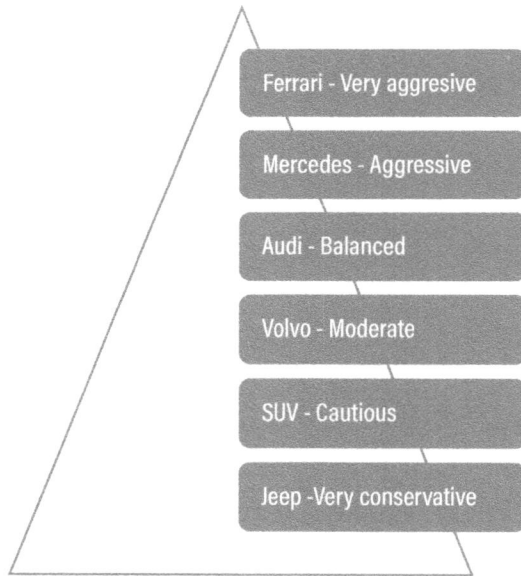

Figure 8. Cars as Risk Profiles

'I want you to place these cars in your portfolio instead of placing them in your garage. Your retirement savings are a long-term investment, so you invest in an aggressive growth fund, which is like the high-performance Ferrari. Money for the world trip with children is invested in a growth fund, which is like a moderately aggressive Mercedes. Your goal for having your own business is invested in a moderately conservative fund like the Volvo, and you keep your emergency funds and any goals for the next 12 months in cash at the bank, which is like the Jeep', Mia explained (see Figure 8 and Table 8).

Table 8. Risk Profiles & Asset Allocation

	RISK PROFILE	ASSET ALLOCATION	EXPECTED RETURN ABOVE INFLATION	INVEST- MENT TIME- FRAME
Ferrari	Very aggressive	100% growth	5.8%	At least 7 years
Mercedes	Aggressive	15% defensive; 85% growth	5.2%	5–7 years
Audi	Balanced	30% defensive; 70% growth	4.9%	5 years
Volvo	Moderate	50% defensive; 50% growth	4.1%	3–5 years
SUV	Cautious	70% defensive; 30% growth	3.4%	3 years
Jeep	Very con- servative	100% cash	1.9%	N/A

Note: Data supplied by the MLC Capital Markets Research Team. Please note that historical investment outcomes are no indication of future investment outcomes.

Asset allocation is simply allocating your investment into different assets—cash, FI, shares and property—to balance risks and rewards. In general terms, the higher the potential return of an investment, the greater the risk.

RISK MANAGEMENT STRATEGY

Start Early

'Is it a good time to invest now?' Richard asked. 'Because I am hearing too many rumbles. The news media keeps saying that the recession is coming and the market may crash any time soon.'

'Let me show you an example: two friends, John and Peter, decided to invest $500 per month, which is $6000 per year. John got started at age 18, once he found his first full-time job; he kept investing for eight years and then stopped adding money at age 26, as he got married and had too many commitments. However, he kept investing without withdrawing his investment. His investment became $69,928 in eight years.'

Mia showed Richard and Lisa the tables that depicted the numbers. 'John's money then compounded at a rate of 9 per cent per year, which is roughly the average return from Australian shares in the last few decades. By the time he retires at 67, how much does he have? He has **$2,761,964**.'

'But, his friend Peter began investing the same amount—$500 per month—at age 27. Peter keeps investing $500 every month until he is 67 years old. For 39 years, his money also compounded at 9 per cent a year. When he retires at age 67, he is sitting on a nest egg of **$2,134,203**. The total amount he invested is $234,000, which is five times more than the $48,000 that John invested!'

'Why does Peter ultimately have less money than John? John never invested anything after the age of 27,' Lisa asked.

'Because he started earlier than Peter. The compound interest that he earns on his investments adds more value to his account than he could ever add on his own. Compound interest is the addition of interest to the principal sum of investment; it is interest on interest. The real secret to riches is to set aside a portion of your money and invest it so that it compounds over many years. That is how you become wealthy while you sleep', Mia explained (see Table 9).

Table 9. Compound Interest

AGE	JOHN	PETER
19	$6254	
26	$69928	
28	$83,663	$6254
37	$187,499	$82,742
47	$459,626	$299,586
57	$1,126,708	$831,150
67	**$2,761,964**	**$2,134,203**

Note: Amount invested = $500/m ($6000 p.a.); rate of returns = 9% p.a.; compound frequency = monthly

'We are in our late 30s. Is it too late to start for us?' Richard asked anxiously.

'When did you start contributing to your superannuation?' Mia responded.

Richard thought back. 'I started working at age 14, so I guess my job started contributing to my superannuation when I was a teenager.'

'You have superannuation with a balance of approximately $185,000, and Lisa has $70,000. You have a combined superannuation balance of $255,000. If you want to retire in 20 years and start contributing $25,000 per year each, then your super fund will receive a yearly contribution of $21,250 from each of you. Every dollar you contribute to your superannuation needs to pay 15 per cent tax if you earn less than $250,000 per annum. If your superannuation compounds at 9 per cent after fees and tax, you will ultimately have $3,603,430 combined after 20 years. If you decided to work five years longer than you planned, your money would grow to $5,798,674 combined in 25 years', Mia explained to the astonished couple.

Table 10. Richard's and Lisa's Super with Compound Interest

TIME	RICHARD	LISA
Current super balance	$185,000	$70,000
10 years	$760,812	$488,565
20 years	**$2,123,969**	**$1,479,461**
25 years	$3,395,164	$2,403,510
Combined balance in 20 years	$3,603,430	
Combined balance in 25 years	$5,798,674	

Note: Super contribution = $21,250 p.a. after 15% tax; compound interest after tax and fees = 9 per cent compounding yearly

Diversification

In terms of investment, a common metaphor that is used is to not place all your eggs into one basket. No one type of security, asset class or investment manager provides the best performance over all periods. The reasons why a diversified portfolio works are because there tends to be more 'winners' than 'losers' over time and because the investments that gain money offset the ones that go bust.

Investors should consider diversifying their portfolios based on the following specifications:

- **Type of investment**—Investors should include different asset classes, such as cash, bonds, shares and properties. They shouldn't forget to account for lifestyle assets that they already have. As an investor, if you already own a home, then investing in another residential property would be poor diversification.

- **Markets and regions**—As an investor, if you invest in just one company's shares or in a bunch of shares in the same industry, investing for the long term will not render your portfolio any safer. Consider asking someone who only held Enron shares or e-commerce shares for years; their value vanished overnight. Spreading your exposure within each asset class across numerous countries, currencies and industries ensures that your investment is not narrowly concentrated in a particular region or industry.

- **Investment management style**—Different investment management styles tend to excel according to different economic and market conditions. This allows you, the investor, to benefit from the expertise of several managers rather than simply relying on one investment manager.

- **Timing**—'Timing risk' is the chance that your investment will suffer due to the time when you buy and sell your investments. Dollar–cost averaging will help investors reduce timing risk.

TAX-SAVING STRATEGY

'We are paying lots of tax every year. Is there any way to minimise tax? Our accountant suggested that we should buy an investment property and save on tax from negative gearing', Richard asked.

'Nine out of 10 of my clients want me to help them save tax', Mia replied with a smile. 'However, tax saving should not be the main reason for investing. Tax benefits are intended to encourage you to act in a way that the government wants, but the government's reason should not be your reason for investing. Why do you think the government introduced some policies like negative gearing to encourage investment in property?'

Looking at their confused faces, Mia continued, 'It is because one of the main sources of taxation revenue for the Australian government is from tax on property—stamp duty, rates, land tax and capital gains tax from sales are all taxes people have to pay if they want to own or sell property'.

Richard and Lisa looked at each other and nodded.

'So your investment strategy should be based on your own goals and needs so that the possibility of achieving them can be maximised', Mia added. 'But, we will consider tax-effective investment strategies, which generate sufficient returns and help you more quickly achieve your goals'.

'If you want to reduce your tax liability, you need to reduce your spending first', Mia instructed.

'Reduce our spending to save the tax?' Lisa repeated, sounding confused.

Mia explained, 'The more you spend on your lifestyle, the more tax you have to pay. You should understand that you pay most of your bills and shopping with your after-tax income. Your employer deducts your income tax from your pay and pays it to the government, while you pay another tax—the 10 per cent goods and services tax (GST)—for most of the goods and services that you purchase. This is tax on top of the tax on your spending. When you consider different investment options, you will notice that the interest from savings at the bank does not have any tax benefits. However, when you consider investing in growth assets—such as shares and property—there are tax benefits. If you contribute more to your superannuation for retirement, there is a very generous tax break'.

Tax-Effective Investments

'You mentioned tax-effective investment strategies. How do they work?' Richard asked.

'Tax-effective investment signifies that you pay less tax than you would on another investment with the same return and risk. A lower tax can help your investments grow faster. Knowing what marginal tax bracket you are in for your ordinary income is a good method for understanding how tax affects you', Mia explained. 'How much did you earn for the last financial year before tax?' Mia asked Richard.

'My last year's income before tax was approximately $150,000', he replied.

'Your marginal tax rate is 37 per cent because your income is in the range of $120,001–$180,000. If you earn extra dollars, you usually need to pay 37 per cent tax on that income. If you can invest in a way that allows you to pay less tax on your investment returns than 37 per cent, then you're ahead', Mia explained.

Table 11. Income Tax Rates 2022/2023

INCOME THRESHOLDS	RATE	TAX PAYABLE ON THIS INCOME
$0–$18,200	0%	Nil
$18,201–$45,000	19%	19c for each $1 over $18,200
$45,001–$120,000	32.5%	$5,092 plus 32.5% of amounts over $45,000
$120,001–$180,000	37%	$29,467 plus 37% of amounts over $120,000
$180,001 and more	45%	$51,667 plus 45% of amounts over $180,000

Note: Australian income tax rates for 2022/2023, excluding Medicare levy (residents)

'How can we get ahead?' Lisa wanted to know.

'The income you receive from shares and property—dividends or rent—will generally be taxed at your marginal tax rate. However, Australian shares that pay fully franked dividends can be a tax-effective investment because a 30 per cent company tax would already be paid if the dividend was fully franked. You pay comparatively less tax with a franked dividend than with an unfranked dividend', Mia explained.

'Another profit that you can receive from your share and property investment is capital gain. When you dispose of your investment for more than what you paid for it, you make capital gain and need to pay capital gains tax (CGT). If you hold the investment for more than one year, you will receive a CGT discount, and you will have to pay tax on half of your capital gain. So, Richard's marginal tax rate is 37 per cent and your capital gains are only taxed at about 18.5 per cent', Mia replied.

Children's Education Fund

'We would like to save for our children's college funds in 10 years. We both have a high marginal tax rate, so can we invest under our children's names to save the tax?' Lisa asked.

'No', Mia replied. 'Any investment income over $416 for someone who is younger than 18 years old will be taxed up to 66 per cent. It is much higher than an adult's marginal tax rate. For example, if you invest $30,000 with investment returns of 3 per cent per annum under your children's names, then the investment income per annum will be $900. The first $416 is tax free, but income between $417 and $1,307 will be taxed 66 per cent. Assuming your investment return is 5 per cent per annum, then the total income $1,500 will be taxed by 45 per cent.'

Table 12. Tax Rates for Residents Under 18
(excluding Medicare Levy)

INCOME	TAX RATES FOR 2022/2023 INCOME YEAR
$0–$416	Nil
$417–$1,307	66% of the excess over $416
Over $1,307	45% of the total amount of income

'Youths under the age of 18 are paying a higher tax than adults? Are all the incomes for minors taxed that high?' Richard asked.

'No. The income from employment, business and a deceased estate for minors will be taxed by normal adult marginal rates. The penalty tax rate for the youth is to avoid people investing under their names to pay fewer taxes', Mia replied.

'What is the best method of investing in our children's education expenses?' Lisa asked.

'One of the options that you can consider is an insurance bond. It is a tax-effective way of saving for your children's education', Mia replied.

'Insurance bond? Is it an insurance product?' asked Lisa.

'It is a combination of a managed fund and an insurance policy. It is a life insurance policy, so there is a need to nominate a life to be insured, as well as a beneficiary. However, the investment works much like a managed fund. You can choose an investment option from low risk to high risk and the value of the insurance bond will rise or fall based on the investment market', Mia explained.

'Insurance companies pay up to 30 per cent tax (corporate tax rate), so you do not need to pay extra tax, so long as you hold the bond for at least 10 years. Your marginal tax rate is at 37 per cent, which is higher than the 30 per cent of insurance companies, so it is tax effective for you', Mia explained.

'If we access the bond before 10 years, do we need to pay extra tax?' Lisa further asked.

'Yes, you need to pay the difference between your 37 per cent marginal tax rate and the 30 per cent tax rate paid by insurance companies—or you need to pay the portion of the difference, depending on the year from which the withdrawal was made', Mia said.

'Can we add the money to the insurance bond like a managed fund does?' Richard asked.

'Yes, you can. There is a certain rule that you need to follow, though. Your contribution cannot exceed 125 per cent of the previous year's contribution', Mia explained.

'If we exceed, will we have to pay a penalty?' asked Lisa.

'If you do, then the start date of the 10-year period will reset. You will then have to wait a few more years before you can gain the full tax benefits', Mia said.

Insurance bonds offer a combination of simplicity and security, along with tax benefits and professional investment management. They are an effective tool for high-income earners to save for a child's future or their own future.

There are limitations for the amount of money you can contribute to your super fund each year. If you are 30 years old and want to achieve your financial freedom by age 40, superannuation is not the best vehicle for your goal as you can't access your super fund before age 60. You need another investment structure that gives you a tax-effective income stream when you choose to stop working.

Insurance bonds may provide estate planning opportunities for some investors. If the insured person passes away, then the beneficiary receives the proceeds from the insurance bond, free of tax.

Investment Structures

'Before you have decided how much to invest and in what, you should consider the best investment structure for you to use. An investment structure is the way in which your investments are legally owned. Many people simply purchase assets in their own name or in their joint names in Australia, but other ownership structures may be more suitable. You can use partnership, company, trust and superannuation structures. Which one is the best structure to use depends on your goals and direction', Mia explained (see Table 13).

Table 13. Summary of Ownership Structures

	INDIVIDUAL	PARTNER-SHIP	COMPANY	TRUST	SUPERANNUATION
Income tax	Marginal rate (0–45%)	Marginal rate (0–45%)	25–30%	Assessed at rates of beneficiary	15%; 0% (super fund paying a pension)
CGT	< 12 months; 0–45%; > 12 months: 0–22.5%	< 12 months; 0–45%; > 12 months: 0–22.5%	25–30% (no discount)	Assessed at rates of beneficiary	< 12 months: 15%; > 12 months: 10%; 0% (super fund paying a pension)
Asset protection	No	No	Yes	Yes	Yes
Set-up costs	Low	Low	Higher	Higher	Higher
Income splitting	No	Between partners	Between shareholders	Between beneficiaries	No
Loss distribution	Yes	Yes	No	No	No

Note: Tax rates excluding Medicare levy

'Which one is the best structure for someone who has a high marginal tax rate?' Richard wanted to know.

'Taxation is one of the main reasons that people seek advice regarding the different structures. However, tax should not be the primary reason for determining a structure. You should also consider the protection of your assets, estate planning, risk mitigation and the delegation of control for now and in the future. It can be expensive to fix if this is done wrong, as there are costs for transferring assets from one structure to another. The largest one is CGT because when you transfer your assets or give up a right to something, you may be regarded as having disposed of that asset', Mia told them.

'Asset protection? How does it work?' Richard asked.

'Wealthy people normally do not own anything in their own names—but they control everything. Your assets are at risk if you suffer a claim from a creditor. Asset protection is important to someone who is in a high-risk occupation or to business owners. If Lisa wants to have her own business in five years, you may need to pay special attention to this. Company, trust and superannuation structures can offer you asset protection', Mia further explained.

'You also mentioned estate planning. Are you talking about how to distribute our assets if we die one day?' Lisa inquired.

'Yes. Your assets in your company, trust and superannuation will not form part of your estate, which can be distributed based on your will. So, you should also understand and organise them in a way that reflects your wishes', Mia answered.

Understanding the advantages and disadvantages of each investment structure before you invest has significant long-term benefits. There is no right or wrong structure for everyone—only a right or wrong structure for your goals and future needs.

THE FIVE TYPES OF INVESTMENT STRUCTURES

Individuals

The most common and simplest investment vehicle is a person holding investments in their own name. There are many advantages to investing in the name of an individual:

- It is simple; there are no additional administration times and costs, as well as no set-up costs.
- Income is taxed at a low marginal tax rate (if the person has minimal 'other income').
- The 50 per cent CGT discount applies if you have held the asset for a minimum of 12 months.
- Losses can be offset against your 'other income'.
- You are tax advantaged if the investment is the family home.

The disadvantages of investing in the name of an individual can include:

- There is no asset protection if the individual is in a high-risk occupation and could be sued and have their assets exposed to risks from creditors.

- There is no flexibility with the distribution of income, and income is taxed at rates of up to 45 per cent.

Partnership

A partnership is a contractual relationship between the partners. It is not a separate legal entity and the partners can be individual, companies or trusts.

The advantages for this type of investment structure include the following:

- Set-up costs for a partnership are low, and it is easy to understand and administer.
- A partnership allows some income splitting between the partners. However, the partnership income must be split by the partnership agreement.
- Partners that are individuals or trusts can use the 50 per cent discount on capital gains.

The disadvantages of partnerships can be summarised as follows:

- There is no asset protection in a partnership. The assets belonging to either partner may be subject to creditors' claims, as all partners are jointly and severally liable.
- A partnership lacks flexibility in terms of allocating the income between the partners.

Company

A company is a separate legal entity and it is most often used as a structure for business rather than for investments. The advantages of a company can be summarised as follows:

- Company income is taxed at the relatively low flat rate of up to 30 per cent.
- Companies have limited liability, which offers some protection for shareholders if the business fails or is sued.
- A company has a perpetual existence, and it does not cease to exist if a director or shareholder dies or leaves the company.
- A company can retain profit within the business and it does not have to distribute to shareholders.

The disadvantages of a company can include the following:

- A company has higher set-up costs than other structures, with the requirement for separate set-up accounts and tax returns each year.
- A company cannot claim the 50 per cent CGT discount.
- Losses that are incurred by the company are trapped within the company. Only the company can carry those losses forward. The shareholders cannot use those losses.

A company should generally only act as an investment vehicle when it is the beneficiary of a discretionary family trust, in which case it ensures that the company does not derive capital gains.

Trust

A trust is a popular legal entity that is expressed through the action of the trustee. Beneficiaries are ultimately entitled to receive and retain a trust's income, capital or both. The trustee is generally only taxed on the balance to which no beneficiary is immediately entitled. Trusts are a popular investment structure, but they are often poorly understood. The main types of trusts are discretionary trusts, unit trusts and hybrid trusts.

The advantages of this type of investment structure can be summarised as follows:

- There is complete flexibility with income splitting, which can stream different types of income and capital gains to different beneficiaries who are taxed for the profit at their marginal tax rate.
- The 50 per cent CGT discount is available.
- The trust's assets can be protected in the event of litigation against beneficiaries, as there is no single individual who owns any assets. Therefore, creditors of an individual cannot access any assets that are held by a trust.

The disadvantages of trusts can include the following:

- They are complicated to understand.
- They include moderate set-up and administration costs.
- They cannot distribute losses, which can be carried forward to be offset against the trust's income.

A trust is generally used by individuals who wish to maintain control of their investments and who have the ability to protect their assets and tax-effectively stream the income/capital gains between family members.

Superannuation

Superannuation has been specifically designed so that it can save for your retirement—and its tax benefits render it particularly attractive. It can be a tax-effective method of increasing the wealth for your retirement.

'When you contribute to your super fund, you only need to pay the contribution tax of 15 per cent (or 30 per cent if your income is greater than $250,000 per annum), which is much lower than your marginal tax rate of 37 per cent. Investment returns in super also pay 15 per cent tax. If you invest in something outside super, then you must pay tax on investment returns at your marginal tax rate. There are significant differences in the outcomes between super and non-super investment across year spans. The figures in Table 14 reveal the varying results from 10 to 40 years. Peter invested $500 a month, and it compounded at a rate of 9 per cent a year; he will thus have $753,128 in 40 years, assuming that he pays tax at the highest marginal rate of 45 per cent for his investment. If he invests the same amount of money, which compounds at 9 per cent a year in super, he will save a total of $1,578,150 in 40 years, as he only pays a 15 per cent tax for returns in super. Once he retires, he can move the investment in super to the pension phase, where there is no tax payable for the investment returns, so it's even better', Mia explained.

Table 14. Different Returns between Super and Non-super Investment

TIMEFRAME	SUPER (15% TAX)	NON-SUPER (45% TAX)
10 years	$89,708	$77,434
20 years	$282,024	$204,335
30 years	$694,306	$412,303
40 years	$1,578,150	$753,128

Note: Amount invested = $500/m; rate of return per annum = 9% before tax; compound frequency = monthly.

'But you said that we couldn't access our super before we retire', Lisa objected.

'That's exactly right. Your investments must be a combination of super and non-super investment. You need to take advantage of the tax benefits of superannuation and have non-super investment for your short to medium-term goals', Mia explained.

Superannuation is money that you set aside during your working life so that you will have money on which to live during retirement. The primary purpose of superannuation is to provide retirement benefits, so it is usually not available until you retire.

Whether superannuation is the most appropriate investment structure for you depends on your age, goals and needs. There are more issues to consider than just tax advantages for Richard and Lisa, as they cannot access their super before age 60. Therefore, they must keep some money where they can easily access it. Insurance bonds can provide such a structure for tax-effective investment, allowing early access before age 60.

Self-Managed Super Fund (SMSF)

'We had seen another adviser before we came to you, who recommended an SMSF to us. Is it an option that we can consider for our superannuation?' asked Richard.

'If your super balance is less than $500,000, it may not be cost effective for you to set up an SMSF. There is also a checklist to assess someone who may be suitable for an SMSF besides super balance,' said Mia.

- Do you wish to control your fund's investments and have the financial experience and skills to make sound investment decisions and choose the right investment options for your fund?
- Do you have the time, interest and ability to establish and maintain a fund in accordance with all the various rules and regulations?
- Do you wish to perform the role of trustee or director, which imposes important legal obligations on you?
- Do you have a budget for ongoing expenses—such as professional accounting and tax, audit, legal and financial advice—and wish to keep comprehensive records and arrange an annual audit by an approved SMSF auditor?
- Do you wish to use the flexibility of the SMSF structure to access estate planning, social security and retire-

ment planning outcomes that may not be available through your current retail or industry fund?

After reviewing this checklist, Richard and Lisa both thought that SMSFs were not right for them.

'We want something simple that does not require a lot of time and skills to manage our super fund because we do not have much knowledge at all about investment, or about the government's rules', Richard said.

The Australian Taxation Office regulates SMSFs, which can include up to six members. It is a private super fund and each person manages his or her own fund—which requires great responsibility. Therefore, this investment structure may be for you if you have extensive knowledge of financial and legal matters and want to dedicate all your time and effort to managing your super fund.

* * *

Useful tips for long-term investors include the following:

- **Start early.** You can benefit from compound interest by starting early with your investment. The best way to arrive early at your destination is to start early.
- **Invest enough money.** The fundamental challenge of investing is to invest enough money so that you have a real shot at achieving your goals. A skilled

adviser will focus on assisting people to find ways to do just that.

- **Diversify your investment.** Diversification will not guarantee any gains nor protect against losses. It is about managing the risks/rewards trade-off by selecting a mix of investments that help you achieve more consistent returns over time.
- **Invest in the right things.** Taking too many or too few risks will not help you achieve your goals. If you pick the right investment, then you will reap greater rewards over the long term.
- **Stay the course.** Avoid buying and selling investments at the wrong time just because you became caught up in media hype or fear. It is critical that you control your emotions throughout your journey.
- **Choose your structure of investment.** You should choose the most suitable structure for your investment from the very beginning, as it can be expensive to change later.
- **Know your tax savings.** Understanding how tax works with your investments means that you do not pay more tax than you need to. However, you should never base investment decisions on tax benefits alone.
- **Borrow to invest.** Gearing accelerates your wealth, but it also magnifies your down-market losses. Go through the checklist to assess whether you are ready to borrow for investment and that you fully understand the risks that are involved. You will find more detail in the next chapter.

Chapter 6

ONE SIZE DOES NOT FIT ALL

When Anna introduced Mia, the adviser, to Lisa, she mentioned that Mia's advice was highly tailored to individual circumstances. She told Lisa, 'You know my situation is different from others. Her financial advice not only covered investments, but other areas of my finances that affected me as well'.

Anna is a close friend whom Lisa has known for years—a slim and beautiful ballet dancer who married her husband Michael, an oncologist, 10 years ago. Michael is 12 years older than her and has two grown-up sons from his previous marriage. They had a high level of savings, but they did not know much about investments, so they made the default decisions to buy two rental properties. Michael has some shares with the Commonwealth Bank, West Farmers and Telstra that are worth around $50,000.

When the couple first met with Mia to seek advice, Michael explained, 'I am older than Anna, so I may retire before her. When I retire, I want to make sure that we are financially comfortable enough to fund the lifestyles that we want. Based on what we have now, I doubt whether we can achieve our goals. I want to know if there is any way to accumulate wealth faster'.

'There are some strategies available to you, but we have to assess your suitability for the strategy', Mia told them.

'There are many investment options out there and some of them are too good to be true. I am very cautious about where we put our money because my parents lost their money from a land scam in the past', Anna explained, showing her concern.

In the 1990s, Anna's parents invested their money into buying the land located on an island just off the Queensland coast. The scammers lured unwary potential buyers living interstate to Queensland by offering free flights and accommodation. They took the investors to the island and pressured them to sign a contract on the spot before they flew back home.

Anna's parents dreamed of owning waterfront land and building their holiday home on it. After they purchased the coastal land, they realised that they had viewed and bought land at low tide. As they were from New South Wales, they did not have any local knowledge—the land being sold was either impacted or covered by sea water at high tide. The scammers targeted interstate investors because they were easily deceived in that situation.

INVESTMENT AND SUPERANNUATION SCAMS

In light of the terrible events that Anna's parents experienced, I will highlight the importance of being aware of scams in this section. There have been many Australians looking to get rich through quick shortcuts, who were ultimately scammed. An Australian Competition and Consumer Commission report indicated that Australians had collectively lost $701 million from investment scams in 2021. Investment scams are often so professional and believable that it is difficult to tell them apart from genuine investment opportunities. The most common types of investment scams are investment cold calls, share promotions and hot tips, investment seminars, and opportunities for early access to your super fund.

These scams share similar promises, such as:

- You will be a millionaire in a few years.
- You can make risk-free investments with guaranteed returns.
- You can have above-average returns at little or no risk.
- You can make government-approved investments.

When you are in a possible scam situation, you can check the legitimacy of the person or company who is offering the investment by asking the following questions and checking the legitimacy of their responses:

- Does your company have an Australian Financial Services (AFS) licence and what is the licence number?
- Is the investing prospectus you are offering me registered with the Australian Securities and Investments Commission (ASIC)?
- What company do you represent and who owns the company?

If they cannot answer these questions directly, then they are probably selling you a scam. Doing your own research on the company or business who offers the investment could save you from losing your money. If someone said that you could receive high returns with no or low risk, you need to know that there is no such thing. They may also promise money-back guarantees and downside protection for your investment, which you must be cautious of. Volatile investments with a protection feature always come with extra costs and fees. There is often an associated motivational speaker who claims to be a self-made millionaire and who shares his or her story of financial success at a seminar. You should never commit to any investment at a seminar and always obtain independent legal or financial advice.

Common superannuation scams include promoters who claim that they can offer early access to super funds by transferring your super into SMSFs. You should know that this is illegal, that heavy tax penalties apply if you participate, and that you may lose all your retirement savings. You need to know that you cannot access your super before age 55 (at the earliest), except in very limited circumstances, such as financial hardship or compassionate grounds.

Cryptocurrency scams lead the way, and scammers claim to have developed highly profitable trading systems based on special algorithms and fake celebrity endorsements.

ACCELERATED WEALTH WITH GEARING

'You said that you wanted to build your wealth more quickly. There is a strategy called gearing—it involves you borrowing money to invest. It can help you achieve your goals faster', Mia explained to Anna and Michael. 'Actually, you have already borrowed money and invested in properties so you are doing that now—but we need to do it with the right strategies if you want to accelerate the growth of your wealth. The borrowed funds have to be productive enough to earn a higher return than the costs of investment, including interest; this is similar to what banks do in their business', Mia explained.

'Similar to what banks do?' Anna repeated, raising her eyebrows.

'Yes. Banks borrow money from us at lower interest rates and then lend the funds to property mortgages and businesses at much higher interest rates. That is how banks make billions of dollars in profit', Mia illuminated with a smile.

'So, you want us to think like banks', Michael summarised.

'If your money is sitting in a savings account at the bank, others will use it to make their profit. For exactly the same reason, you can use bank money to grow your own wealth, which is also much faster than simply using your own money', Mia responded.

'There are two friends—Betty and Sally—who both invest $100,000 of their savings in a high-growth managed fund, which generates a 10 per cent positive return. Sally is a more aggressive investor, so she invests $100,000 of her savings and another $200,000 of borrowed money with a loan interest of 7 per cent in the same high-growth managed fund. A year afterwards, Betty's investment grows to $110,000 and her investment return on capital is 10 per cent. Sally's investment becomes $316,000 after loan interest payments and her return on initial capital is 16 per cent. Ten years later, Betty's investment grows to $270,704, while Sally's investment becomes $812,112, with a compound interest of 10 per cent. The returns on capital for Betty and Sally are 171 and 372 per cent respectively, after all the costs of borrowing are accounted for', Mia detailed.

She focused on Anna and her husband before adding, 'The combination of gearing and compounding help you build your wealth much faster'.

'I can see that', Michael replied, with a certain twinkle in his eyes (see Table 15).

Table 15. Scenario 1—Gearing v. Non-Gearing with Gains

ONE YEAR	BETTY	SALLY (GEARING)
Own investment	$100,000	$100,000
Borrowed money	$0	$200,000
Total investment	$100,000	$300,000
Return of investment, 10%	$10,000	$30,000

Interest payments, 7%	$0	-$14,000
Investment value with return	$110,000	$316,000
Net profit	**$10,000**	**$16,000**
Return on capital	**10%**	**16%**

TEN YEARS	BETTY	SALLY (GEARING)
Own investment	$100,000	$100,000
Borrowed money	$0	$200,000
Total investment	$100,000	$300,000
Total investment in 10 years, with compounding of 10% monthly	$270,704	$812,112
Interest payments, 7%	$0	$140,000
Net profit	**$170,704**	**$372,112**
Return on capital	**171%**	**372%**

'Borrowing to invest magnifies the gains, but do not forget that it multiples the losses too. You need to fully understand both the potential benefits and the risks of this type of strategy', Mia cautioned.

She further added, 'Betty and Sally have had a bad year this time, with a negative return of 10 per cent. Betty's investment becomes $90,000 and the loss of capital is –10 per cent. However, Sally's investment drops in value by $30,000 and she needs to pay the interest of the loan, $14,000. The value of investment becomes $256,000 and her loss on capital is –44 per cent'. (See Table 16.)

Table 16. Scenario 2—Gearing v. Non-Gearing with Losses

ONE YEAR	BETTY	SALLY (GEARING)
Own investment	$100,000	$100,000
Borrowed money	$0	$200,000
Total investment	$100,000	$300,000
Loss of investment, 10%	–$10,000	–$30,000
Interest payments, 7%	$0	–$14,000
Investment value after loss	$90,000	$256,000
Net loss	**–$10,000**	**–$44,000**
Loss on capital	**–10%**	**–44%**

'But you are not going to have negative 10 per cent returns every year. The share market will eventually pick up', Michael argued. 'I bought CBA shares with $25 in 2009 during the GFC, and the share price has increased to $100 per share today. I regret that I didn't buy more.'

Mia nodded at his remark. 'I call it a Boxing Day share sale. Buying the down-market shares, combined with the gearing strategy and compounding, will accumulate your wealth much faster than you could ever imagine', she affirmed.

WHO IS SUITED TO GEARING?

'There is a checklist that you can use to gauge whether borrowing to invest is right for you', Mia mentioned.

The checklist for gearing includes the following questions:

- Can you sleep at night if your investment performs poorly?
- Will you invest for the long term—for at least seven years?
- Do you have enough surplus income for the loan repayment if the loan interest increases or if you receive a margin call? (More details about this will be shared later in this chapter.)
- Do you have a high marginal tax rate to make the most of any tax benefits?
- Is your strategy flexible enough to allow for changing circumstances, such as having children or a drop in your income?

'What you have to first consider is your risk profile and the timeframe of your goals. Will you be able to sleep at night if your investment drops in value by 30 or 40 per cent or more? Will you be able to follow the strategy for more than seven years?' asked Mia, directly following the questions from the checklist.

'Why is it for that long?' Anna asked curiously.

'Gearing is a long-term investment strategy that usually has a seven to 10-year time horizon. This is because the growth assets will outperform in the long term, but they are volatile in the short term. In regard to paper assets such as shares and managed funds, if you do not sell in a bad market, then it is just a paper loss. However, once you have sold your investment in a down-market, a loss on paper becomes a real loss', Mia explained.

'The second important factor that we must consider is your cash flow and cash capacity. You must have a very strong cash flow to service the loans during the time that you invest, as well as the capacity to input more cash if the interest rates increase,' she added.

'We are the couple with no children and no plan to have any children in the future. Our cash flow is strong and we have plenty of surplus every month. Michael does not need to pay child support anymore because both his sons from his previous marriage are now adults', Anna responded.

'The third factor you should be aware of is a tax implication in gearing, as the interest of the loan for your investment is tax deductible. I know both of you are paying high taxes, especially Michael with his highest marginal tax', Mia continued.

Gearing is an effective tool for filling the gap between your goals and current resources. It is appropriate for clients who have aggressive risk profiles—younger investors are also potentially suitable, as they do not rely on the income from their investments. These conditions would generally exclude older investors, such as retirees.

NEGATIVE AND POSITIVE GEARING

'Our two properties are negatively geared. Our accountant told us that we could save on tax that way', Michael said.

'Tax savings should not be the main reason for investing. As I mentioned before, banks make huge profits from borrowing low and lending high. You build your wealth from using a gearing strategy only when the returns of investment are greater than all the costs of borrowing. If your investment is negatively geared, then the interest on the loan and any other expenses with the investment property are more than the rental income received. You only change this loss situation when you sell the house and make a profit. Otherwise, it will always be a loss. How are your investment properties doing?' Mia asked.

'One of them is a house that has increased a lot in value in the last few years and the other one is a townhouse that is not doing as well,' Anna replied.

You will often hear that investment is 'negatively or positively geared'. However, what does this actually mean?

Negative gearing: This is when expenses that hold an investment, including the interest repayment, are more than the income received, which results in a loss situation.

Positive gearing: This involves income from the investment that more than covers all the expenses that relate to the investing, which results in a profit situation.

A loss from negative gearing can be used to reduce your taxable income, and additional net income from positive gearing must be taxed. However, with negative gearing, if you cannot make a capital gain when you sell your investment, you will eventually make a loss. Tax deduction is thus not the main reason for investment.

'Let me ask another question, Michael. If you suddenly stop working and there is no income coming in, can you still keep the negatively geared investment properties?' Mia asked.

Michael thought about the answer. 'With Anna's sole income, it will be hard to keep both of them. We would have to sell', he replied.

'Investment that costs money from your pocket will not provide you with the security and freedom that you seek. Only positive cash flow from your investment can do that for you. So, your investment must be positively geared to eventually provide you with financial freedom', Mia explained.

BENEFITS AND RISKS OF BORROWING TO INVEST

Both benefits and risks are involved in a gearing strategy. Borrowing to invest can include the following advantages:

- It offers you more money to invest, and you can build your wealth much faster.

- There may be tax benefits if you are on a high marginal tax rate, as you are usually allowed a tax deduction for interest payments on the loan.
- If the investment is positively geared, you have access to a passive income stream that can help take you one step closer to your financial freedom.

Although the benefits of borrowing to invest are attractive, gearing can magnify losses as well. The greatest risk is derived from the fact that you are investing in something that you do not fully understand. Having a separate exit plan before considering this type of strategy is essential. The risks that you must consider include the following:

- **Investment income risk**—The income that you receive from the investment may be lower than expected. For example, a company may not pay a dividend or a tenant may default. Do you have funds set aside to cover this scenario?
- **Interest rate risk**—The interest rates on loans could rise. If they rose by 2 or 4 per cent, could you still meet the loan repayments?
- **Income risk**—What if your income stops due to sickness, injury or redundancy? Do you have a plan to manage this?
- **Capital risk**—The value of your investment may fall and the proceeds from the sale may not cover the remaining loan balance. Do you have other funds set aside for managing this eventuation?

If you want to build your wealth faster with a gearing strategy, then you must both understand and feel entirely comfortable with each risk. The more you borrow, the higher the risk, as you will have to repay the loan regardless of the investment's performance. Having enough surplus or savings and sufficient personal insurances to mitigate these risks should be part of a sound plan.

COMMON GEARING STRATEGIES

There are a few common gearing strategies available. It is recommended that you discuss them with your financial adviser in regard to their suitability based on your needs.

Real Estate

This is our most familiar gearing strategy, and the real estate may be a home or an investment property. Anna and Michael purchased investment properties with borrowed money and they hope that their values will increase over time. If all of your investment money is tied up with one or several investment properties, this would constitute a poor diversification.

Equity Lending

Equity lending allows the borrower to utilise equity in your assets so that you can obtain a loan and invest. The most common form of equity lending is a home equity loan. Anna and Michael do not have a mortgage against their family home, but they do with their investment properties. They can borrow against their family home or the difference between the market value of their investment properties and the amount that is still outstanding on their investment loan. The borrowed funds can be used as a deposit on an investment property or they can be invested into shares or a managed fund.

Instalment Gearing

Instalment gearing combines an investor's own funds with borrowed funds to regularly invest in a portfolio, which would thus build wealth over time. I mentioned dollar–cost averaging in the previous chapter, which includes a combination of dollar–cost averaging and gearing strategy.

Instalment Warrants

Instalment warrants are products with built-in gearing. They are traded on the ASX with a gearing level that typically lies between 20 and 60 per cent.

Instalment warrants allow investors to buy investment products, such as shares, in a series of instalments. The initial payment provides the investor with access to the product's benefits (e.g. dividend payments), but the investor does not have ownership rights. The outstanding balance on the instalment warrant is treated as a loan—with an interest component and a borrowing fee—which is usually included upfront in the initial payment. To obtain a fully paid share, the investor must make the final payment. If the share price has fallen below the amount of the final payment, then the investor can walk away from the loan.

Internally Geared Funds

Internally geared funds are gaining traction among investors' managed funds and ETFs. All the internally geared funds borrow internally to fund their investments by using both the investor's funds and the borrowed funds. The investor does not borrow the money to invest; the fund itself borrows and is responsible for all gearing obligations. As is the case with all gearing, internally geared funds will magnify both positive and negative returns.

Another common gearing strategy is margin lending, which will be discussed in further detail later in this chapter.

Gearing can be considered an effective strategy only if the after-tax capital gain and the income return of the geared investment exceed the after-tax costs of funding the investment. Gearing is considered an effective long-term strategy because growth-based investments deliver higher potential returns over the long term. However, you should be fully aware of the volatility of this type of investment and have the necessary funds available for managing any debts involved.

SHARES V. PROPERTY

'I bought those shares a long time ago. The share prices are up and down and I keep them. The dividends are good and I reinvest most of the dividends these days. We bought those two investment properties soon after we moved to Brisbane. During the property boom in the pandemic, the value of the house I bought more than ten years ago doubled, and we have a steady rental income from both properties. Some people made good money from shares, and I would certainly like to explore more. However, with my job, I do not have the time to understand complex investments or trade shares myself', Michael told Mia.

'You have a large exposure to properties and I think it is time to diversify your investment. Shares and properties both help you increase your wealth and generate more income', Mia responded. 'There are both advantages and disadvantages when it comes to investing in shares and properties with borrowed money. The most obvious advantage is that property finance is easier and cheaper than shares finance. However, shares can reinvest dividends and grow more quickly with compound interest. If you want your property to increase in value, you can facilitate this with renovation and improvement.'

'One of the worst problems of property is liquidity', Mia stated.

'I agree with you. When you need money, you cannot sell a bathroom or a bedroom', Michael nodded his head in agreement.

'The disadvantage of shares is high volatility. People feel that the price of shares can vary wildly from one day to the next due to the ease with which they are bought and sold', Mia explained.

'Owning real estate is a more tangible investment—one that you can see and touch. It can thus bring more security and stability', Anna said.

'However, owning property can be more complicated to manage than owning shares', Mia added. 'You can diversify into both shares and property because they both offer you capital growth and income. At times when the share market underperforms, the property market is likely to ensure more consistent stability in regard to returns. However, when you need money, shares will offer you the flexibility to access your money quickly', Mia stated.

Table 17. Reasons for Investing in Properties and Shares

INVEST IN PROPERTY	INVEST IN SHARES
Potential for significant capital growth	Potential for the greatest capital growth
Regular and frequent rental income	Potential for regular dividend income
Secure hedge against inflation	Ability to outpace inflation
Numerous tax benefits	Tax befits from franking credit
Greater degree of control	Higher potential returns
Lower volatility	Lower entry, holding and exit costs
Brick and mortar—more tangible	High liquidity and an easy start
High demand for property	Diversification
Higher leverage	Ability to leverage
Cheaper finance	Reinvest the earnings and benefit from compound interest
Increase in value from renovation	

PROPERTY SECURITIES

An alternative method for investing in property without having to outlay large amounts of capital and entry or exit fees is through the use of property securities. This is a property managed fund in which you can own numerous properties, such as residential, commercial, retail and industrial properties. Managed property security funds spread investors' risks, as they provide more diversification and are liquid. Property securities have both income and capital growth, but they tend to generate higher returns in income than in capital growth.

WOMEN AND MONEY

Maggie is Lisa's aunt and she is a divorced single lady in her 50s. She is a registered nurse with Queensland Health, as well as a hardworking woman. She owns a debt-free house and recently received an inheritance $300,000 from her late mother. She has been a risk-averse person since she lost her investment with Storm Financial in 2009.

Storm Financial was a financial advisory business with more than 13,000 clients across Australia. Maggie and her ex-husband were advised to draw on the equity in their investment property and apply those funds so they could obtain margin loans for buying shares. This created a gearing-on-gearing (double gearing) situation that would substantially magnify the risk of loss. When the market rose, they made good money before the GFC. But a serious problem commenced in 2008 when the share market started to crash. This triggered margin calls on their portfolio, and they had to deposit additional cash or sell the shares at the worst time. When they reached the point at which they could no longer reduce their borrowings and meet margin calls, they lost their investment property.

'We lost our investment property during that crash. This had many effects—it also greatly pressured our marriage, and we divorced after a few years. I saw many older people lose their homes during the GFC. We were in our 40s at that time and we still had time to recover. I am in my 50s now, so I can't afford to take high risks anymore', Maggie explained, when she met with Mia for the first time.

Margin Lending

Before the GFC, margin lending was becoming an increasingly accepted method of wealth accumulation. It was not classified as a financial product by ASIC at the time, so it was not regulated. From December 2005 to December 2008, the value of margin loans that were outstanding in Australia had approximately doubled to $41 billion, but as at June 2018, the loans outstanding were reduced to $11 billion. Margin loans were then defined as regulated 'financial products' on 1 January 2010, and advice on margin lending is now regulated by ASIC.

The Storm Financial collapse affected many retirees who should never have been advised to use margin lending at that stage of their lives. A margin loan lets you borrow money to invest and uses your shares or managed funds as security. Margin lending is an effective gearing strategy—but only if you fully understand the risks and how to manage them.

As we know, shares and managed funds fluctuate in line with market movements. To gauge the risk of their loans, lenders use a loan to value ratio (LVR). The LVR is the amount of your loan divided by the total value of your shares. Most lenders require that you keep the LVR below a maximum of 70 per cent.

As an example of LVR, Maggie had $200,000 invested in a managed fund and had borrowed another $300,000 to invest by using a margin loan. This provided her a total portfolio of $500,000. She had a loan which was 60 per cent of the value of her portfolio and had an LVR of 60 per cent, which was close to the maximum borrowing limit of 70 per cent mentioned previously.

Margin Call

When the value of her portfolio fell during the GFC, Maggie's LVR increased. When her loan exceeded the maximum LVR—70 per cent—she had to either top up her investment or repay some of the loans to lower the LVR back to an acceptable level. This is known as a 'margin call'. If your LVR is very close to the maximum borrowing limit, you will have a higher chance of being required to make a margin call.

To make a margin call, she had to find extra cash to pay the lender or offer the lender additional security by investing more. If you have some money to buy shares at a Boxing Day sale to reduce your LVR with your margin loan, it will perfectly fit this investment strategy—that is, you should buy low. Otherwise, you have to sell part of your investments at a market low, which creates a loss. That was what happened to Maggie during the GFC.

Benefits and Risks

It is essential that you understand both the benefits and risks that are involved in margin lending. The benefits can include:

- **Faster wealth creation**—Borrowing to increase the size of your investment portfolio can allow you to increase your wealth at a more rapid rate.
- **Ability to borrow without the need for property equity**—People generally borrow money using their homes as equity. Margin loans can be borrowed without property equity, instead using the value of shares as security for the loan.
- **Diversification**—A larger portfolio that uses borrowed funds can provide greater diversification.
- **Tax effectiveness**—You may be able to claim the interest on your loan as a tax deduction and receive greater dividends with attached franking credits, which may further reduce your tax liability.

Conversely, the risks of margin lending can include:

- **Loss from investment**—You may face huge losses if the market falls, and you may be forced to sell part of your investment at a low price to meet a margin call.
- **Change of LVR**—If the lender decided to lower the maximum LVR for one of your investments, you would then receive an unexpected margin call.
- **Risk of security**—You could lose your home if you borrow against it for the investment.
- **Borrowing costs**—Borrowing costs may increase if the lender decides to increase the interest rate.

In light of the benefits and risks discussed above, here are some tips for managing margin loan risks:

- **Borrow conservatively**—The first rule of margin loans is to borrow conservatively. This means that you should borrow much less than the maximum LVR that the lender offers and that you should never mortgage your home to invest in a margin loan.
- **Diversify**—Ensure that you choose a diversified managed fund or a diversified portfolio of shares.
- **Pay the interest**—Most margin loans do not force you to make regular repayments, so the interest can just be added to the loan. Making regular repayments can prevent your debt from increasing each month.
- **Check your LVR ratio regularly**—Check your loan account regularly because the value of your investment can quickly change if market circumstances also change.
- **Have cash or security ready for margin calls**—If the lender makes a margin call, you will have to respond very quickly, usually within two to five days, or maybe less during a volatile market environment. Assuming that your portfolio dropped to 50 per cent, ask yourself whether you have enough cash or security to top up. If you do not, then you will need to sell your investment. Prepare for the worst.
- **Shop around for the best loan**—Margin loan interest rates and features vary, so ensure that you shop around for a lender that suits your specific needs. Some margin loans do not have margin calls, but you need to pay both principal and interest.

Ensure that you seek advice from a qualified adviser.

Margin lending is suitable for someone who understands how it works and who has enough cash to meet the margin call if the market falls. A trusted adviser should be able to tell you if you are right for this type of gearing strategy, as well as teach you how to manage the risks.

When Maggie finally came to meet with Mia to seek advice, her finances were very disorganised. She had not even completed her tax returns for three years, and her death benefit primary beneficiary with superannuation was still her ex-husband. She had no idea about where she was financially or what she was capable of achieving.

'After my ex-husband and I separated five years ago, my mum got sick. My brother was in Perth and I was her only daughter, so I looked after her. She passed away one-and-a-half years ago. I was completely worn out and didn't consider my finances much at all. When I was married, I was efficient at budgeting, saving and dealing with credit cards. However, my ex-husband, Patrick, was the one who handled more complex issues like investing. He invested through the margin loan—and I had no clue that he was doing so', Maggie admitted, sighing with regret.

The financial wellbeing of women in retirement is a significant and growing concern. Based on figures from the Association of Superannuation Funds of Australia, a woman retires today with an average of $157,050, while a man retires with a balance of $270,710. The main reasons provided were that:

- Women are paid less than men in Australia. Australia's national gender pay gap has hovered between 14 and 19 per cent for the past two decades.
- Many women are working part-time; currently, 46 per cent of working women are also the primary carers for their children and for ageing parents. This severely affects their retirement savings.
- Women are still taking a backseat in money matters and leave financial decisions to their spouses and partners.

The fact is that once they are in retirement, women tend to live longer than men. An argument can be made that money for women may need to last longer. Regardless of whether you are happily married or single, it is still imperative that women plan for their financial future as independent women.

The financial security of single women is of great concern, and older single women are the fastest-growing demographic of homeless people in Australia, due to family breakdowns or the death of a partner. Many widows confront years of undue financial hardship after their husbands die. Most of them have received little or no life insurance benefits after the deaths of their husbands, as they never discussed financial planning or the possibility of life alone.

Separation is a highly emotional and traumatic period in a woman's life—one that significantly impacts a whole family's financial wellbeing. Most people drastically underestimate the effects of separation, so it is important that women in particular learn how to handle their finances independently.

'It took me five years to recover economically after my divorce. I had to start all over again, and now I have just paid off the mortgage and received mum's inheritance. I need to determine what I will do in the next phase of my life and I need to set up a solid plan for my future', Maggie confided in Mia.

Twelve months after she engaged Mia's adviser services, she had organised all her important money matters. She finalised her tax returns for the last three years, allocated her inheritance into different investment accounts with which she felt comfortable, in regard to her risk tolerance level, and she persistently works towards her retirement goals.

'I was embarrassed to tell anyone and I was not in the right mental state to plan my own finance. I don't know what I don't know and I had no confidence at all to manage my own money. Asking for assistance from you is the best financial decision I have ever made after my divorce', Maggie said appreciatively.

* * *

Today, women are better educated, more successful and more ambitious than ever before. Having confidence in your ability to plan for a better future is critical for financial wellbeing and living the life of your dreams. That confidence is derived from education and experiences that you use to take action and make small steps.

A financial adviser is your planning partner who helps you make these plans and dreams a reality. A financial adviser is also an educator who helps you understand what is involved in meeting your future goals and dreams. Regardless of whether your dreams involve another person, you cannot make your dream a reality by simply relying on someone else's efforts and resources. You need to ensure one thing—a man is not your financial plan.

Chapter 7

YOUR BEST RETIREMENT

Brian and Wendy, Richard's parents, were in their early 60s and were considering retirement in the next five years. They did not have many other assets except for their family home, with a small mortgage of $50,000 and their super. They came to see Mia with encouragement from their son.

'So, we want to know where we are placed for our retirement now. We want to retire in the next few years, but we do not know when we will be ready, or how much we will need. Is it too late to start?' Brian asked.

'It's never too late to start', Mia said encouragingly.

She drew a horizontal line on a whiteboard beginning with '1' and ending with '10'. She then asked Brian and Wendy, 'How confident are you right now that you will be able to retire when you want, with as much as you will need, on a scale of 1 to 10 where one is the least confident and 10 is the most confident?'

Mia handed the pen to them, and Brian and Wendy marked number two on the line.

'We are not confident at all', they admitted. 'We have no idea if we are on track for our retirement', Wendy said, with Brian nodding.

'Retirement planning is not as complicated as you might think. Once you know how much income you need, for how long and where it originates from, you can determine whether your retirement planning is on track', Mia explained.

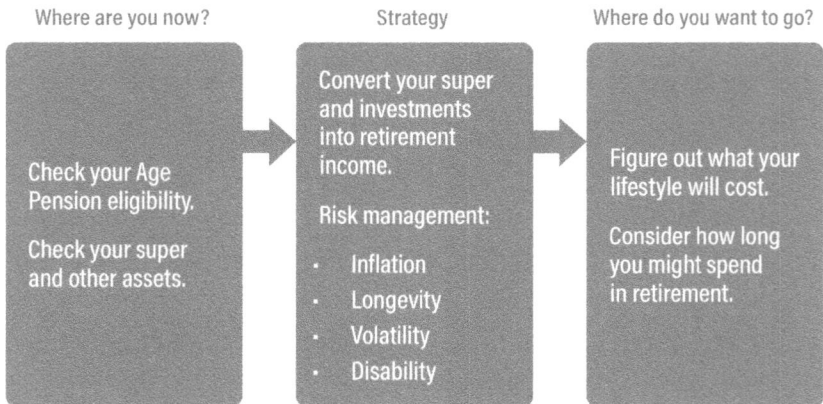

Where are you now?	Strategy	Where do you want to go?
Check your Age Pension eligibility. Check your super and other assets.	Convert your super and investments into retirement income. Risk management: · Inflation · Longevity · Volatility · Disability	Figure out what your lifestyle will cost. Consider how long you might spend in retirement.

Figure 9. Retirement Planning

HOW MUCH DO YOU NEED
FOR RETIREMENT?

'What is the purpose of money for you?' Mia asked.

'Well, I guess we want to be comfortable when we retire', Brian replied.

'Ok, but let's go further. What does a comfortable retirement mean to you?' Mia asked, hoping to elicit a deeper response from her clients.

'We want to maintain our lifestyle, not worry about money all the time, and be able to do something nice for the children and someday—hopefully—for the grandchildren', Wendy replied.

'Sounds good. Now, please tell me more about how you visualise your life in retirement in 10 years, 20 years, and beyond, as well as where the money will come from', Mia instructed.

'We haven't thought that far. We may downsize the house in a few years and move into a retirement village, finding what to do when we retire along the way. Wendy may want to work one or two days a week, but it all depends on the availability of work. We do not know how much we need, but we have heard that you need one million to retire comfortably', Brian said.

'Yes, many people may have offered that million-dollar figure, but there really is no magic number. The amount of retirement savings that you need will depend on your circumstances, financial resources (both inside and outside super) and your lifestyle. Based on the Association of Super Funds of Australia (ASFA) retirement standard, you need approximately $68,000 p.a. to live in a comfortable retirement as a couple. To have this level of income, you do not need $1 million—you only need $640,000 retirement savings, assuming you have 6 per cent investment returns. Do not forget the Age Pension. You may receive full or a part of your Age Pension when you retire, and you need to top up with super funds for the shortage', Mia explained.

Table 18. Savings Amounts Required to Support a Modest or Comfortable Retirement

CATEGORY	SAVINGS REQUIRED AT RETIREMENT	ANNUAL SPENDING IN RETIREMENT, AGE 65	ANNUAL SPENDING IN RETIREMENT, AGE 85
Comfortable lifestyle for a couple	$640,000	$68,014	$62,237
Comfortable lifestyle for a single person	$545,000	$48,266	$44,851
Modest lifestyle for a couple	$70,000	$44,034	$40,656
Modest lifestyle for a single person	$70,000	$30,582	$28,379

Source: ASFA Retirement Standard—September Quarter, 2022. All figures are in today's dollars, using 2.75 per cent average weekly earnings as a deflator and an assumed investment earning rate of 6 per cent per annum.

'You said that you would like to maintain your current lifestyle, so we should do a proper budget to determine how much you currently spend and how much you expect to spend in retirement. To maintain your current lifestyle, it is normally suggested that you need approximately 70 per cent of your pre-retirement net income. This is based on mortgage costs amounting to approximately 30 per cent of income and your home being paid off before you retire. If you hope to travel overseas significantly more, or you acquire expensive hobbies, you may need more', Mia explained.

'We may need to spend more money on holidays for the first few years', Wendy said.

'In general, there are three stages of retirement, and you may spend different amounts of time in each stage. When you first retire, you are in an active stage and spend more because you might be taking holidays or be more active in your hobbies. Then, you might settle into a simpler lifestyle in which there are fewer costs of living. In the last stage, you have a supported lifestyle and your expenses support your increased health and care costs', Mia explained in turn (see Figure 10).

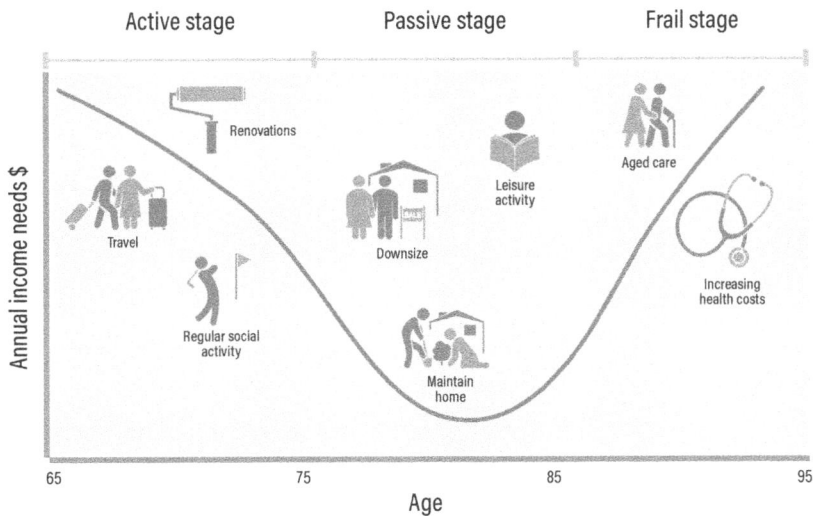

Figure 10. Different Stages of Retirement

The National Seniors Australia report (Kaplan Professional 2017) offers some pointers regarding the key goals for retirees:

- Generate a regular stream of income to meet essential spending.
- Access income that will always be available.
- Meet health and aged care costs later in life.

The financial factors that must be considered when addressing these three goals include Age Pension entitlements, life expectancy, cash flow projections, the sustainability of an investment portfolio, longevity risk and inflation, and potential cognitive decline and aged care.

HOW LONG IS YOUR RETIREMENT?

'I want to retire as soon as possible, but the government changed the retirement age. Now it is age 67', Brian said.

'Yes, if you were born after 1 January 1957, then your new Age Pension eligibility age is 67. But you can retire at any time when you are ready', Mia informed him.

Estimating a desired date of retirement is essential in financial planning, as the earlier you retire, the longer you will have to support yourself. If you retire before the pension age, you will need your own resources—superannuation or non-superannuation—because it has become increasingly difficult to access social security unless you are prepared to seek employment or undergo retraining. With health care and living standards continually improving, you may be retired for 20 years or longer.

'Richard told me that your parents are still alive. How old are they now?' Mia asked.

'Wendy's parents passed away in their 80s, a few years ago. My mum is 85 and my dad is 89, and they are in good health', Brian answered.

'So, you have a good chance of living longer than the general life expectancy', Mia told them. 'You need careful planning to ensure that you have enough money to last.'

YOUR AGE PENSION

'Based on what you currently have, you will most likely receive a full or part Age Pension when you retire. Age Pension is not sufficient for a comfortable retirement, so you need to generate an income stream from your super and other assets to cover your other costs', Mia further explained (see Table 19).

Table 19. Maximum Age Pension Entitlements, Assets and Income Limits as at January 2023

CATEGORY	AGE PEN-SION PER ANNUM	ASSETS LIMITS FOR HOME-OWNER	ASSETS LIMITS FOR NON-HOME-OWNER	INCOME LIMITS PER FORT-NIGHT
Maximum Age Pension for a single person	$26,689	$280,000	$504,500	$190
Maximum Age Pension for a couple	$40,237.60	$419,000	$643,500	$336

Source: Australian Government Department of Human Services

Whether you are eligible for a full or part Age Pension depends on your income, assets and other factors. The maximum Age Pension (as at January 2023) is $26,689 per annum for singles and $40,237.60 for couples combined. To qualify for the maximum amount, a single homeowner can have assets of up to $280,000, while non-homeowners can have up to $504,500. Homeowning couples can have assets of up to $419,000 (non-homeowners have up to $643,500). Your family home is not included in the asset test.

Single people can have incomes of up to $190 a fortnight, while couples can earn $336 a fortnight combined without reducing their maximum Age Pension entitlement. The Age Pension may provide an additional source of income to help fund your retirement lifestyle.

YOUR RETIREMENT INCOME

Risks of Retirement

'Many people lost large amounts of their retirement savings when the GFC hit 10 years ago. We will retire in the next few years, so we are wondering whether it is a good idea for us to withdraw our super funds when we retire and keep them in a savings account at the bank?' Brian asked, raising his concerns.

Like other people in their age group, security is something that Brian and Wendy hold as a priority in their retirement. It is difficult to feel 100 per cent secure all the time, as very little in this world is guaranteed.

Four major risks that we must address when we retire include:

- inflation
- longevity
- volatility
- disability

Inflation and Longevity

'Can you place your retirement savings in the bank? My answer is no. Your retirement planning is like walking upwards on the escalator that goes downwards, and the journey on the escalator is much like your journey of retirement. The escalator is moving at the rate of inflation. If you keep your money in the bank and receive minimal interest, you will actually move backwards—you will be farther away from your goals. If you climb too slowly with ultra-conservative investments, then you may still move backwards—you are getting farther away from your ideal retirement. That journey on the escalator is extremely long for some people, as they live longer. To make your money last longer in retirement, you must climb faster than the rate of inflation', Mia explained.

Australia is currently experiencing a high level of inflation as a result of the impact of the COVID-19 pandemic, the war in Ukraine, and strong consumer demand. Inflation is one of the investor's worst enemies. Once you stop working, you start to pay more attention to inflation and spending power. The longer you live, the more you experience the influence of inflation. The key will be to earn returns in excess of inflation.

At 3 per cent inflation, $1 million in today's dollars will be worth:

- $744,093.91 in 10 years from now
- $553,675.75 in 20 years from now
- $411,986.76 in 30 years from now.

People want to have a stable level of income in their retirement, so being able to estimate life expectancy is essential. In the 1980s, life expectancy at retirement averaged about 74 years of age. Now, it is 85 years for males and 88 years for females, based on the Australian Life Table 2014–2016, by the Australian

Bureau of Statistics. If you are a couple, there is a 33 per cent chance that one of you will live to 94.5 years of age.

It is also essential to recognise that 50 per cent of people live longer than these averages. So, although the statistics are a good starting point, you cannot assume that they will reflect your circumstances. We can only predict life expectancy based on one's health situation and family history. Uncertainty about the timeframe for your retirement is one of the largest challenges, and we must develop strategies that can help your money last longer.

Volatility

Risk management during pre-retirement is different from that in retirement because one must draw income from his or her retirement savings. Sequence risk is somewhat like dollar–cost averaging, but in reverse. With dollar–cost averaging, you would invest regularly and buy more investments when the investment cost is down. When you are accumulating wealth, a negative return early on in the share market works to your benefit as you buy more shares. When you retire and withdraw income from your investments, you are selling your investment regularly, not buying. You must thus sell more investment to obtain the same level of income in the down-market.

'Here is a good example of sequence risk. Two retirees, Bob and Sue, each start with $1 million in an account-based pension and draw an income of $60,000 per annum, indexed to inflation of 2.5% per annum for ten years. Right after Bob retired, there was the GFC, and he had two years of negative returns for his account-based pension. Sue had two years of negative returns at the very end of a 10-year period, rather than at the beginning. Let's take a look at the outcomes for Bob and Sue over 10 years. Bob's account balance is $615,275, which is much lower than Sue's account balance, $860,339. They both have 5 per cent average returns for their pension after ten years', Mia said.

'Why is it so different after ten years if they receive the same pension payments and the same average return?' Brian asked curiously.

'It is because of sequence risk. If there is a bad market just after you retire, then your investment may never recover, but if you retire in a good market, your retirement savings may grow large enough to make your money last longer. Sometimes it is a matter of luck, but you can't simply rely on luck at retirement. There are some strategies that limit the downside risks, which I will explain later', Mia stated.

Table 20. Comparison of Sequence Risk

Financial Year	BOB Return (actual)*	Amount	SUE Return (swapped)	Amount
2008	-6.4%	$876,000	9.8%	$1,038,000
2009	-12.7%	$703,248	8.7%	$1,066,806
2010	9.8%	$709,129	0.4%	$1,008,036
2011	8.7%	$706,210	14.7%	$1,091,604
2012	0.4%	$642,806	12.7%	$1,164,008
2013	14.7%	$669,414	9.6%	$1,207,868
2014	12.7%	$684,847	2.8%	$1,172,107
2015	9.6%	$679,272	10.4%	$1,222,685
2016	2.8%	$625,187	-6.4%	$1,071,329
2017	10.4%	**$615,275**	-12.7%	**$860,339**
Average	5.0%		5.0%	

Source: MGD Wealth
*Actual median Australian balanced superannuation fund return

Investing for retirement can be a little like running a marathon. You want to avoid as many obstacles as you can as you try to reach your retirement goals. In a marathon, hills and headwinds will slow your performance; in retirement, market fluctuation, inflation and other factors such as tax will hinder your performance. Investing to overcome those hills and headwinds will help you reach your goals much more quickly.

RISK MANAGEMENT IN RETIREMENT

'There is no silver bullet for all the risks that we have talked about before, as everyone has different needs. However, there are some good strategies (e.g. the bucket strategy) and products that provide a level of protection against a down-market and inflation. We normally use a combination to meet individual client's needs', Mia explained.

'How does the bucket strategy work?' Brian asked.

'Say you have $500,000 in your super and you want to draw $30,000 a year to top up your Age Pension. If your risk profile is 30 per cent defensive and 70 per cent growth, then we invest $60,000 in cash to cover your payments for two years, and $90,000 in fixed interest, which is a low risk and low returns investment. We invest the rest ($350,000) in growth assets, such as shares and properties, which may have a higher element of risk and returns', Mia explained.

'But the rest of the $350,000 is still invested in a volatile investment', Wendy clarified.

'The benefit of the bucket strategy is that you are not forced to sell a volatile investment (e.g. property or shares) when the market is low just because you have cash and FI to cover immediate living expenses. It is also a good strategy for managing the sequencing risk that I mentioned previously', Mia explained.

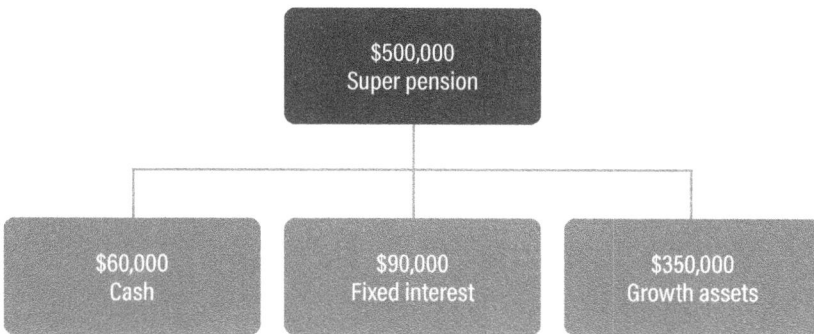

Figure 11. The Bucket Strategy

Withdrawing early on during the 'bad' years could deplete the portfolio before the 'good' years arrive. Many advisers use the bucket strategy to avoid taking distributions from asset classes, such as shares, during the down-market. The bucket strategy, paired with simple rebalancing, offers a sound plan for generating cash flows in retirement. With rebalancing, the investments that are up the most are sold, and the ones that are down the most are bought instead to maintain initial asset allocation. The retirees consequently use the following framework to manage their retirement savings:

- If the shares are up, they take retirement spending from shares.
- If the shares are down but the FI is up, they take the spending from FI instead.
- If both shares and FI are down in the same year, they take the distribution from cash.

But the limitation of the bucket strategy is that a conservative cash bucket typically provides two to three years' cash for an investor to draw down on before they must start selling FI and growth assets. If the market hasn't returned within that period, investors need to sell FI. After they sell all FI, they then have to sell growth assets.

In light of this information, you may ask yourself how you can minimise risk without sacrificing returns. There are some other risk management strategies at retirement:

- **Diversification**—Diversification at retirement can be different from the accumulation phase, as you would require an income from your investment. You must have a portion of your money allocated to defensive assets and you had better draw from this portion during the 'bad' years. However, you would still need to invest part of your money into the growth assets to have returns that are higher than inflation.
- **Professionally managed products with a dynamic approach**—There are products that have the flexibility to adapt asset allocation as needed. For example, the fund managers move your investment to more defensive assets, such as cash or FI, if they detect a high risk in the market. Your investments are thus continually positioned to manage the risk of large losses, as well as potentially deliver real returns during numerous market conditions.
- **Investment protection**—This offers a protected retirement income for a fixed period (term) or life and it is available as a feature on account-based pensions. It allows you to invest your

retirement savings in a way that increases your investment so that you can make your money last longer. However, if the market falls, then your retirement savings will be protected, and you will continue to receive an income for the rest of the term or for life.

- **Focus on your retirement goals**—When you buy growth investment assets such as shares and property, you expect some short-term volatility, so it is vital that you do not panic when markets drop. Trusted advisers will help you manage the risk of the market and will advise you whether the assets you hold are still appropriate for achieving your long-term goals.

CONVERT TO RETIREMENT INCOME

The Australian retirement income system is based on three pillars—the Age Pension, your superannuation and your assets outside superannuation. It includes a fourth pillar, if you wish to downsize your family home. Assets held outside super funds might include investments in properties, shares or term deposits, business assets and trusts.

An investment strategy for when you work full-time may need to change when you retire. An important consideration when retiring is how to invest all your savings and assets so that you can replace your wage with regular income when you are retired. These assets must be managed to try to balance the three key needs of retirees:

- Income needs—retirees want certainty of income
- Longevity needs—retirees want to ensure that their retirement income lasts
- Capital needs—most retirees want flexibility in accessing a lump sum during retirement for numerous possible needs.

'There is no single investment product that meets the three key needs of retirees, so we may need to use a combination of them. You may also wish to adjust your investment risk to ensure that you have enough money to last throughout your retirement—but also that you have enough to earn sufficient returns so that inflation will not reduce your retirement savings over time', Mia explained.

The main retirement income streams include:

- Account-based pensions
- Annuity
- Other investments.

Account-Based Pensions

A superannuation pension that we consider an account-based pension is the primary type of income stream available in today's market. It can only be purchased with money that is held in superannuation. It is one of the most tax-effective methods of investing your retirement savings, as the income payments and investment earnings that you receive are generally tax free if you are aged 60 or over. With a superannuation pension, you can choose how to invest your money—and your money can subsequently grow. However, investment earnings will vary based on economic and market conditions, and there is a minimum amount that you must withdraw each year. The risk management strategies that I mentioned above can manage risks more effectively with an account-based pension.

Annuity

An annuity is an investment that pays a series of regular guaranteed-income payments for either a fixed period or for life, which can meet retirees' longevity needs. It may be purchased with superannuation funds or with non-superannuation money. If superannuation funds are used, the income payment receives the same tax treatment as superannuation pensions do. With traditional lifetime annuities, you are protected from negative market movements, but you generally will not benefit from any positive market performance. Once established, the amount and frequency of the income payment may not be altered. However, there are currently market-linked annuities whose income streams are linked to the performance of investment markets.

Other Investments

Account-based pensions and annuity are popular as income streams in retirement because they have the benefit of tax concessions and exemptions. However, you can also place your money in a term deposit, in an interest-bearing account or in other investments such as shares, investment properties or managed funds.

Keeping your money in a term deposit or in an interest-bearing account are two ways of ensuring that you have the flexibility to access your money for emergency purposes or capital needs. If you have all your retirement savings at a bank, the value of your savings will not keep up with inflation. Before the GFC, the term deposit rate was almost 8 per cent. If you had a retirement balance of $1 million, you would live comfortably off that amount. However, there has been a general fall in official interest rates since the GFC, both in Australia and overseas. Best-rate term deposits fell to just 2.0 per cent in November 2019 and increased to 4 per cent in January 2023. Based on Canstar, this dollar income is not sufficient in the high inflation environment. Consequently, retirees have had to either compromise their standards of living or they have had to significantly draw down their capital to meet their costs of living. Drawing down on capital creates the risk of running out of money, as well as the inability to fund a 20-year and longer retirement (see Figure 12).

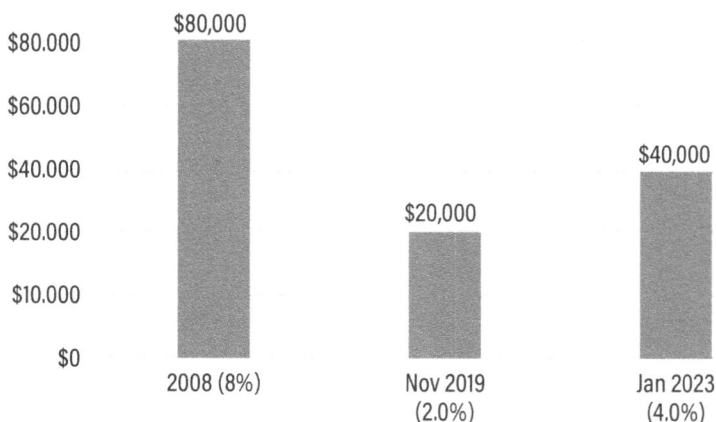

Figure 12. Falling Term Deposit Income

Downsize Your Family Home

Many people believe that downsizing their family home and buying a smaller place simplifies their lives and reduces their home maintenance and utility costs for many years. You can free up cash by selling the family home and by investing it in shares, term deposits, managed funds or superannuation—which generate an income stream for your retirement.

As of 1 January 2023, if you are aged 55 or over and you sell the principal residence that you have owned for at least 10 years, you can contribute up to $300,000 to your superannuation from the proceeds. Couples can contribute $300,000 each.

However, selling your home may affect your Age Pension entitlement, so you should consult with a financial adviser on the subject of social security implications and investment options of the proceeds.

CLARITY AND HOPE FOR RETIREMENT

'Once you know what you need and what you have, this exercise offers you clarity for your retirement. There is a gap between what you want and what you have now, but we can work on this over the next few years. Your financial plan will show you all the recommendations for filling the gap, and lifelong cash flow modeling. That is a financial planning tool showing you in projection if you can achieve your desired lifestyle with the recommended strategies. It is a very effective tool assisting you to accumulate enough wealth to generate sufficient income at retirement, ensuring you don't run out of money before you run out of life', Mia said.

'We have a much clearer picture of our retirement now. When we came to see you, we did not know where to start, but I feel that we have hope now', Brian replied, with Wendy nodding in agreement.

'You will begin viewing your retirement income as not just a means of paying the bills, but as a means of funding your life—the life that you want', Mia explained. She pulled out the original confidence metre and said, 'I want you to go back to this confidence metre with the same question that I asked you at our first meeting. After our discussion, how confident are you about your retirement now on a scale of 1 to 10?'

'I think that we are standing at nine now. We realised that there is a gap that we need to fix, but we know that there are options and strategies available to us to help us improve, along with your help', Brian answered.

DESIGN YOUR RETIREMENT

'When would you like to retire?' Mia asked.

'Tomorrow!' Brian answered impatiently. 'I would like to retire as soon as possible. Once we retire from work, we can do lots of things that we love. Since the restructuring at work they have changed management and there are now many issues. They have a different approach for everything, so it is becoming more difficult as a result.'

Why have so many people given their lives to work they do not enjoy? Because they need the money. We claim that we save money so we can retire from work and have a life one day. Not all of us need $1 million or more in assets and investments to have the life we desire. It is important to understand this and be prepared so that you retire to something you enjoy and feel passionate about, not just to get away from work you don't like.

You hope for a life of ease when you retire, but you may have a life of boredom instead. Retirement planning has been mainly focused on the financial challenges that are found in retirement; however, quality of life and a sense of emotional wellbeing become important elements of retirement. Non-financial problems that people experience when they retire include:

- **Loss of identity**—You have been Professor Henry for 30 years. Who are you now?
- **Loss of control**—You used to tell people what to do and when to do it. Now it is hard to get a plumber to come to your place for a repair.
- **Boredom**—Are you looking in the garage for something to break so that you can have something to fix?
- **Loss of social connection**—What if you actually miss the boss that you used to hate?
- **Lack of mental stimulation**—Smartphones and smart ATMs are just too smart to understand.
- **Domestic issues**—Your partner does not look happy to have you around all day.

This is a time of life in which people can rethink how they wish to spend the new one-third of life that they have received. It is also the perfect time in your life to switch the primary focus of your life from earning a living to chasing your dreams', Mia told Brian and Wendy.

All the money in the world cannot make a difference for those who feel discontentment and emptiness because their lives are unbalanced. The good news is that in retirement, you will have plenty of time to pursue your dreams. The bad news is that you may have too much time. How would you like to invest your time and money so that you are achieving what is most meaningful to you as an individual? (See Figure 13.)

Figure 13. Your Best Life at Retirement

Ask yourself George Kinder's three questions that were mentioned in Chapter 3:

- What would you do if you had all the money you needed?
- What would you do if you had five to 10 years left to live?
- What would you do if you had one day left to live?

Self-inquiry is a powerful method for discovering what we really want in our lives. Answering the question relating to 'all the money you need' helps you uncover what really interests you and what makes you feel alive, without money restrictions. If you have a full life already, you will feel fulfilled, whether you would die today, tomorrow or in 10 years. However, if you have a list of last wishes, then you need to work on them now.

Successful retirement involves balancing all facets of life in the journey—your family, recreation, community service, health and fitness, and personal growth. The funds that you have been saving so diligently for your retirement are valuable only because they add value to the quality of your life. After all, you have been preparing for life, not just for retirement.

AGED CARE

Other risks retirees face can be the events that threaten their wellbeing, such as ill health. You need to proactively prepare for your future health, as the costs for care can be expensive.

'How are your parents going? Are they able to manage independently?' Mia asked Brian at one of their review meetings.

'My dad had a fall a few weeks ago and my mum feels too overwhelmed to look after him—we know that she is not young either', Brian answered with concern.

'Look, Brian; I think we need to start planning for your dad's aged care', Mia said.

'Do we? What options do we have?' Wendy asked.

Brian's father, Mark, had a fall at age 90 and his health declined rapidly after the fall. Brian and Wendy went through home care and residential aged care options with Mia. They decided that Mark would move into an aged care facility that was close by and that they liked. They had been asked to pay a refundable accommodation deposit (RAD) of $550,000 to secure a place for Mark. Brian was worried, as neither his family nor his parents had this amount of cash available, and they did not want to sell Mark's family home, since his wife, Sarah, still needed to live there.

'There are also other fees for aged care, and I do not know if they have sufficient cash flow to meet the day-to-day aged care expenses', Brian told Mia.

'Yes, they also need to pay daily fees and means-tested fees if their assets are over certain limits. But he does not have to pay the RAD $550,000 upfront in full', Mia told Brian.

After assessing Mark and Sarah's full assets and income situation, Mia prepared their financial plan, which included:

- exploring different options for Mark to pay the RAD
- outlining strategies to increase Mark's Age Pension, reduce the aged care means-tested fee and maximise their cash flow to cover all ongoing care costs for Mark
- restructuring their assets and creating sufficient cash flow to cover Sarah's living costs.

After a few months, Mark moved into the aged care home with confidence, knowing that they had Mia's assistance and enough cash flow to cover all the costs.

As Australia's older population grows at an unprecedented rate, the needs for aged care advice have increased accordingly. People should consider their aged care in advance, but they often ignore it until an incident occurs. The point of time when parents are in hospital and the family is together is essentially the only time that people talk about aged care. Many aged care decisions are made in the carpark of the hospital—but unplanned discussions can result in families making poor choices because they base them on emotions instead of reason.

DIFFERENT TYPES OF CARE

Aged Care Homes

Aged care homes are available for older people when they can no longer live at home and when they need help living safely, healthily and comfortably.

The types of aged care homes in Australia include:

- furnished accommodation
- hotel-like service that provides meals, laundry, socialising and maintenance of the property
- care services that include personal care, such as help with bathing, eating, taking medications, carrying out health treatments and performing clinical care (which provides for medical and therapy services).

The Australian government subsidises several aged care homes in Australia, which makes care more affordable. However, private aged care homes do not receive subsidies from the Australian government.

Every aged care home has differing prices within a prescribed limit. The three different costs involved include:

- a basic daily fee that people must pay, which has a maximum limit of $56.87 per day
- accommodation costs that vary depending on an income and assets assessment
- a means-tested care fee that varies depending on an income and assets assessment. If you need to pay it, the exact amount will be determined once you enter care.

Home Care

One aged care service that is available to people aged 65 and older is home care, which assists people as they remain at home. Many people want to stay in their own home because they value familiar and comfortable surroundings.

Help at home is different for different people. It may signify receiving help with shopping and cooking, or it could involve receiving personal care to help with bathing, dressing and moving in and out of bed. It may even signify receiving modifications that improve your safety and movement around the house. It's important to understand what fees you may have to pay, how much the government will contribute, and how your budget works before you choose your provider.

Your Home Care Package budget sets out the total amount of funds available for your use. It is made up of the Australian Government's contribution and your contribution. What you need to pay depends on your services and your financial situation.

Your contribution towards your Home Care Package could be made up of the following fees:

Basic daily fee: This is an amount that everyone can be asked to pay and varies from $10.49/day to $11.71/day depending on your Home Care Package level. If you provider does not charge this fee, you will have less funds available in your budget to pay for your care, as it is added to the government subsidy to increase the funds available to you in your care budget.

Income-tested care fee: This is an extra contribution that some people pay based on their individual income. If you are a full pensioner with an income of up to $30,204.20, you will not pay an income-tested fee.

Additional services fees: This is something you directly agree with your Home Care Package provider to pay for additional care and services that wouldn't be covered by your Home Care Package budget.

Short-Term Care

Short-term care provides care and support services for a set period—which can range from a few days to a few months at a time, depending on your needs. It offers the carer a break from their service, if he or she is the husband or wife caring for the person, because that can be extremely exhausting, and can even affect the carer's health.

The Australian government subsidises short-term care providers directly so that care is more affordable. You are expected to contribute to the cost of your care if you can afford to do so. How much you pay would vary depending on the type and level of care and services that you will receive. The maximum amount you could be asked to pay is:

- $11.26 per day, if you receive care while living at home
- $54.69 per day, if you receive care while living in a residential setting.

(Please note: all figures in this section on aged care are current as of January 2023, or as otherwise referenced.)

* * *

People must confront ageing so they can create sufficient plans for managing it efficiently. Financial advisers can help people determine their finances so that they obtain the most suitable package. Financial advisers also help clarify their clients' confusions regarding how to use their money for aged care. People are unsure of what the government can supply and what they themselves must provide, as well as the direction they should be heading towards and how quickly or slowly help can be implemented. A high–net worth individual may express unwarranted concern regarding the releasing of his or her financial position to the government when they apply for short-term care, and they need directions to help them navigate the system. Financial advisers educate their clients and help them prepare aged care plans in advance, as well as advise their clients regarding growing their networks and links to other providers in the aged care sector, which would enable smooth transitions into clients' frailer years.

Chapter 8

THE ONGOING JOURNEY

Mia told Richard and Lisa at their first meeting, 'What I am looking for with my clients is a long-term business relationship. If you want to achieve the outcome that you are aiming for, we had better meet on a regular basis. Perhaps we could initially meet every six months, until your finance is in order, and then possibly once a year, based on your needs. If we do not meet on a regular basis, you cannot update me with any changes in your circumstances, and I cannot adjust your plans and strategies according to changes in your circumstances either. A critical part of my job is to keep you accountable and to ensure that you stay on track with your goals. Do you feel comfortable with this plan for ongoing assistance and regular meetings?'

Mia received her answer when Richard and Lisa engaged her in an ongoing service agreement as their adviser. Financial planning should not be viewed as a one-off event, but as an ongoing process.

Financial plans alone benefit no one unless they are implemented. You must have heard the saying that 'knowledge is power'. I disagree; knowledge is a power only when you use it and act on it. Most people know how to become fit—eat more healthily and exercise more often. However, this does not mean that they utilise the knowledge. This is not a knowledge problem; it is an execution problem. Financial fitness is the same.

The barrier between you and the life that you are capable of living is a lack of consistent actions directed towards your goals. A great plan needs effective implementation with the help of an adviser. It involves a long process, but you are not alone.

Richard and Lisa committed to their plan and after 12 months they had their first review meeting, which took approximately an hour:

- They discussed the changes to the couple's circumstances. Richard received a pay rise at work and Mia advised him to direct that money into their repayment of bad debt—their car loans. They paid off their credit cards before the due date to avoid paying any unnecessary interest fees. They moved into their new house, which was closer to the school that their children attended—but the price that they paid for it was similar to the value of their previous home, so they did not take out an extra mortgage.
- They reconfirmed their goals and objectives and tracked their progress against their projected plan. In the previous 12 months, they had auto-

mated the distribution of their surplus funds into different buckets to achieve their primary goals, and they set up protections and estate planning. Their adviser, Mia, had observed the progress that the couple had made so far and highlighted what needed improvement.

- Mia also provided Richard and Lisa with an update on economic conditions, investment markets and any legislative changes.

When they talked about share market movements, Mia said, 'I have a small hobby farm and planted some vegetables. If I am so concerned about how the radishes are growing that I dig them up daily and check the root, can you guess what I will ultimately have?'

'Wilted radishes?' Richard answered, with a small chuckle.

'You are absolutely right. Both vegetables and investments need time to grow', Mia stated.

When they were discussing their possible expenses in the future, Mia said, 'Whenever you make a large payment for anything, ask yourself: is this taking me nearer to my primary goals, or is it leading me further away from them? If this expense does not move you closer to your goals, then you should try to defer or consider alternatives'.

* * *

In her fourth year as their adviser, Mia received an urgent phone call from Richard: 'I saw the news and the share market is crashing. It already dropped more than 20 per cent in the last few weeks. What do we need to do? Can we have a meeting with you?'

'We can have a meeting immediately. But Richard, before the meeting, do not try to sell anything, you hear me?'

'Ok, I will follow you.'

Mia saw the nervousness on their faces when she next met with them.

'You don't need to be in panic. We are just in the bear market', she explained.

'Bear market?' Lisa asked.

'Yes. When the value of the market falls by 20 per cent or more from its peak, we call it a bear market. If the market has risen by 20 per cent or more, we call it a bull market. A fall between 10 and 20 per cent is considered a market correction', Mia explained.

'There have been more than 10 bear markets since the 1970s in Australia; on average, they happen once every four or five years. At your age, you could easily live through at least another seven or eight bear markets in the future. The largest one I remember is the GFC. It was the worst financial crisis since the Great Depression, and we had 54 per cent share market falls.

The market hit rock bottom on 6 March 2009. Do you know what happened next? The All Ordinaries Index surged by 46.8 per cent over the next six months. All Ordinaries present 95 per cent of the value of all shares that are listed on ASX. It thus very much reflects the Australian share market's movements. We had a very similar experience at the beginning of the COVID-19 pandemic in 2020. One moment, the market was falling. In the next moment, one of the largest bull markets in history began. All bear markets are followed by a strong bull market, and it continuously occurs—not just in Australia, but worldwide. Bear markets never last. If you understand the patterns and rules of the game, then investment becomes much easier', Mia explained.

She added, 'It means that now is the time to buy. Do you still remember what I told you before about Boxing Day sales—about purchasing shares when they are on sale?' Mia asked with a smile.

'You had a return of 18 per cent in your portfolio last year. I warned you to not be too excited with a bull market just because you happened to be in the right place at the right time and made some money through sheer luck. As Warren Buffet once said, 'A rising tide lifts all boats ... only when the tide goes out do you discover who's been swimming naked'. A bull market is followed by a bear market this time.'

A good adviser helps eliminate certain emotions that can lead to buying and selling at exactly the wrong moments. In good times, the adviser protects you from greed, and in a bad market, he or she protects you from fear—as well as from unrealistic expectations you may have throughout. Therefore, the main reasons that you should have an adviser are to reduce the risk of investing and to wring the emotions from your financial decision-making.

* * *

In their sixth year working with Mia, Richard and Lisa had achieved most of their five-year goals, except for one: Lisa's dream of having her own coaching business in five years. During the review meeting, Mia said to Lisa: 'Congratulations on your achievements in the last six years. We have accomplished most of the goals that you set. Lisa, when you first came to see me, you wanted to have your own coaching business in five years. We made a plan to prepare for that, and I think you have enough money to start your own business. What is stopping you from taking the next step?'

'Well, I feel like I am not ready yet. I have seen many people struggling in that industry, so I haven't decided to take the plunge.'

Mia responded, 'When you want to try something new, fear tends to hold you back. However, it is a privilege to follow your dreams and take action to achieve them. You will have a good chance of being successful. Even if you do not achieve your goal, it is better to try because disappointment is temporary, but regret lasts forever'.

People usually regret the things that they have not done, rather than the things that they have done. Most dreams will die unachieved if we do not explore them with someone who can help us articulate what we want, as well as assist us in mapping the path to completion.

Six months after that meeting, Lisa resigned from her job and started her own home-based business. She experienced several ups and downs, but she finally began acquiring her own regular clients, as well as referrals from her existing clients.

She followed her adviser's advice in several areas, from setting up her business structure, to managing cash flow in her business, and even personal spending.

Mia had told her early on, 'Once you are established, you may be making more income than you were earning before. But the flow of income may not be regular. It would be better to pay yourself a wage and have separate bank accounts for business and personal spending. Again, budgeting is the key here. You must learn to live with your wages, and do not try to dip into the business account too often. You also need to set aside money for your income tax, to avoid paying any penalties for late tax payments. You may also need to set money aside for GST once your business is registered for that.'

'Yes, I realised that it was different from working for someone else. I need to oversee everything myself', Lisa said with a sigh.

'When you work for someone else, the company deducts tax before you receive your pay. You spend the rest of the income. But, when you work for yourself, you pay tax after you deduct your expenses from your income, especially in a home-based business. It is a tax benefit to have your own business, however, a business owner has many extra roles', Mia explained.

'Do I still need all of my insurances? So far, in the first six months since I started my business, I have made much less income than before,' Lisa asked.

'We will review your insurance needs again. Self-employed people have more risks than others because they do not have sick leave or annual leave. Your IP insurance benefits will not be affected by your reduced income because you applied based on the agreed value of your income with your previous job', Mia told her.

Lisa started making profits from her business from year two, and she wanted to reinvest most of her profit into the business. Mia did not agree: 'This is a common mistake for most small business owners. They normally make a decent income while working, but they have very little to live on in retirement. Do you know why? It is because they try to rely on selling their business to fund their retirement. However, their business may be worth less than they think without their involvement, or it can be too hard to sell. We need to build a separate pool of money for your financial freedom—that is your superannuation and investment portfolio.'

Regardless of your ultimate goals, every business owner needs an exit plan. When do you need to think about and plan your exit strategy? When you start your business. For you, and many other business owners, your business is your biggest asset and your retirement plan. However, simply relying on selling your business to fund your retirement may not always work out every time. If you want to exit your business and retire with true wealth one day, building a money-making machine needs to be included as a part of your exit strategy.

Four years after starting her business, Lisa was able to make twice as much income as she had made in her previous job. She also had more flexibility to arrange her time between work and family, which was one of her original dreams.

* * *

In their tenth year of working with Mia, Richard's role became redundant due to restructuring. He had been in his senior position with the same company for over 12 years, and had received a generous redundancy package, so he and Lisa asked for a meeting with Mia to discuss how to allocate this fund.

Surprisingly, Richard looked confident and calm instead of angry and rejected. He told Mia that he was not worried about finding a new job, since he had years of experience in the industry and great relationships with his peers.

'If it were 10 years ago, I would panic for sure. I had a high level of debt and didn't even have an emergency fund. But we are in a different position now. We paid off all our bad debts and our home loan, and we have investment assets that generate passive income for us. With my redundancy package, I would like to get advice from you rather than treating it as a windfall.

How can we maximise the benefits of our situation?' Richard asked Mia.

'What do you think?' Mia responded.

'I would like to take some time off to recharge myself. I want to take this chance to organise a family world trip for the four of us. It has been on my mind all these years, but I never had the time to do it. I want to take this chance and spend some quality time with my family.'

Mia explained the tax implications with his redundancy package, and the government assistance that he may be entitled to if he couldn't find a job as he planned. She also told him whether his life and TPD insurances would continue when his employer stopped contributing to his super.

As they had already settled their home loan, they decided to keep most of the funds in the high-interest-bearing savings account at a bank until Richard found a new job. They had a three-month trip and visited more than 50 destinations across Europe, Asia, North America and New Zealand. They returned with renewed energy and a new set of mental filters. Richard felt that he was ready to accept a new challenge. Soon after, he received a job offer from a competitor company offering a similar role to his previous one. They also offered him substantially more in base salary and higher commission rates—and he happily accepted. He and Lisa invested the rest of their funds into both super and investments, according to their adviser's recommendations.

Transitioning across job situations or personal relationships can yield a perfect time for self-exploration. You can learn more about yourself and what makes you truly happy and fulfilled.

* * *

In their thirteenth year with Mia, Lisa called her one day and told her that she had just been diagnosed with skin cancer—a malignant melanoma on her leg—and that she would be undergoing urgent surgery to remove it. Mia immediately contacted the insurance company and lodged a claim for both trauma and IP insurances.

After her surgery, a biopsy revealed that further surgery was required. It was a stressful time for her family. But, with the help of her adviser and an insurance company case manager, Lisa claimed for both trauma and IP. She paid her medical expenses with her trauma insurance benefits—$200,000—and covered family living expenses with IP monthly benefits. This was a great relief during this challenging time, and she did not even need to return to her business due to financial pressure. Thankfully, her results were clear after two further surgeries.

When Lisa first took out her trauma policy with her adviser, she chose the option to have her cover reinstated if she ever needed to make a claim. Lisa could now relax, knowing that she is still covered in case something else happens to her in the future.

* * *

A life transition can be positive or negative, planned or unexpected. Some transitions may be quite dramatic and may happen without any warning—as in cases of critical illness, death in a family, divorce, job loss and accidents. These events can leave us feeling like we are entirely unprepared and that we may be thrown into a personal crisis. Trusting an adviser can help you prepare in advance of those unexpected events, so that you can reduce the damage from the changes and more quickly adapt to new ways of living.

Look back and think about how your own life has evolved to this point. What transitions have you undergone? What transitions do you expect to experience in the next 10 years? The following 20 years? And after that? How do you live the best life you can with the money you have? The only one who can decide what is 'best' is you.

STRATEGIES FOR DIFFERENT LIFE STAGES

There are financial implications for every potential life transition. We must be aware of the best financial tools and strategies to apply during every life stage so that we can create a smooth journey.

The First Income Stage

The start of your working life is a great time to lay a strong financial foundation and plan:

- **Budgeting**—It is a critical financial skill that you must master. Build a discipline in which you live within your means so that you do not fall into a debt trap.

- **Set up an emergency fund and build up your savings**—You can start by saving at least 10–20 per cent of your income every month. This will help you cover any emergencies or other expenses without using credit cards or taking out loans.
- **Obtain basic personal and health insurance**—Life insurance is optional if you do not have dependents, but you must protect yourself in the event of disability and injury. Ensure that you are adequately insured while your premiums are low and while you are in good health. When you are older and have a few health issues, you may not be able to obtain personal insurance.
- **Invest in suitable products**—When you are young, you have a long investment horizon. You must consider the notion of starting to invest early and regularly with some of your savings to benefit from the power of compounding.
- **Superannuation**—Super funds are one of your most tax-effective ways of investing. If you have multiple super accounts, consolidate them into one account to avoid unnecessary fees, and then review your investment options to ensure that they are aligned with your needs.

The Dependents Stage

This is a time when commitments and responsibilities start to increase. Career, children and mortgages could all be coming at once in your life:

- **Build adequate emergency funds**—Review your emergency fund to ensure that it can sufficiently cover your expanded family's expenses and that it can cater to increased commitments.
- **Have adequate personal insurances**—As you now have more commitments, ensure that you and your dependents have sufficient insurance coverage.
- **Buy a home that you can afford**—Do not over-extend yourself on housing; instead, leave more for what you value most. There are trade-offs between short and long-term goals. If you spend too much on lifestyle choices now, it may affect your financial wellbeing in the future.
- **Ensure debt management**—It is a critical function at this stage, as you may have a mortgage and other debts. Try to reduce bad debts immediately and borrow primarily for appreciating assets that will help your net worth increase over time.
- **Invest both in super and non-super**—Growing commitments reduce your available funds for investing. Balance your current and future needs and set your priorities efficiently.
- **Set up estate planning**—Take time to plan how you would like to distribute your estate to your loved ones, even though you feel like you may not need it very soon.

The Pre-Retirement Stage

Later on in your career, your children move into adulthood and the costly teenager years are behind you. You may have some additional discretionary income. Managing your investment is critical in this period, so you should redirect your excess savings towards your retirement:

- **Pay off your debts**—If you are mortgage free before your retirement, then more of your retirement income can go towards what you enjoy the most in your retirement.

- **Contribute more in your super**—Paying off your mortgage first or contributing more in your super depends on your circumstances. When you are closer to retirement, it is important that you invest your super in a way that does not risk your retirement savings and income.

The Retirement Stage

Once you stop working, your primary objective is to generate sufficient income from investment and to control expenses so that you stay within your available income. Budgeting becomes the focus of finances once again during retirement:

- **Maximise your super**—Your super is likely to be your greatest investment asset for retirement. Careful planning is required for maximising income from your retirement savings. Account-based pensions and annuities are two of the primary retirement income products that you may wish to explore.

- **Take advantage of your entitlements**—If you are eligible for the Age Pension, you should try to maximise it. Even if you do not obtain the Age Pension, you may be eligible for other benefits, such as travel concessions, cheaper medicines and reduced council and water rates.
- **Downsize your family home**—If you need additional funds for retirement, you could sell your home and buy a smaller and less expensive place. But your Age Pension may be reduced or cut off, so you should seek financial advice before making your decision.

When we experience the transition from one phase to another, the changes can be challenging and overwhelming because we are facing the future with a feeling of uncertainty. However, times of life transition offer you the chance to explore what your ideal life would be. A trusted adviser can remind you of the hopes and dreams that you once had, but perhaps forgot, and then direct you back on track.

Chapter 9

ESTATE PLANNING

'Estate planning is about what kind of legacy you would like to leave for your children and the other important people in your life. Leaving a legacy can also mean passing down your values and stories, as well as shaping how you want to be remembered. As your adviser, I have a responsibility to ensure that your legacy flows in the right direction', Mia had said to Richard and Lisa at their first meeting.

Estate planning involves developing a strategy that ensures your assets are passed on to your beneficiaries in the most simple and effective way when you pass away. It aims to provide peace of mind for you and your loved ones when you are not around. No matter how young or old you are, if you have assets, children or relatives, it is critical to ensure that you have all the necessary legal documents signed and ready should the need arise.

'As someone with no children, that is important for me, too. There was a case like this not long ago in Queensland. When a young couple got married, the husband's parents bought a house for them. The young couple tragically died in a car accident during their honeymoon and had no estate plan in place at the time of their death. As they did not have any children, all of their assets—including the house—passed to the wife's parents because it was deemed by law that the older one of the couple had died first. The husband was two years older than his wife, so all the assets passed from him to her, then to her next available kin—her parents', Mia said.

'It is so unfair for the man's parents. If we died without a will, what would happen?' Lisa asked.

'If you die intestate, that is, without a will, your assets will go to the government, and they will decide how they will distribute them. Most likely, those assets will return to your family, but that will take a long time and they will be distributed according to law, not to your wishes', Mia explained.

A 2015 study, jointly compiled by the University of Queensland, Queensland University of Technology and Victoria University, found that 59 per cent of the population currently have a will in Australia. There has been an increase in disputes over wills in the past decades—up by 52 per cent in New South Wales and 73 per cent in Victoria.

The study revealed these major concerns for Australian families:

- Estate planning can be intimidating and complex to everyday Australians.
- How do we retain family assets in the bloodline?
- Adult children may fight over assets.
- Who will be responsible for the care and financial future of young children?
- How do we protect vulnerable beneficiaries from losing their inheritance?
- Children who are spendthrifts have behavioural issues or addictions.

The checklist in Table 21 on the following page will help you quickly assess your current level of estate planning.

Table 21. Self-Assessment Checklist

TOOL	DESCRIPTION	HAVE	NOT SURE/ REVIEW	DON'T HAVE
Will	A will is the first step in estate planning. It is a legal document that specifies how and to whom you would like to have your assets distributed at the time of your death.			
Enduring Power of Attorney	It appoints someone to make financial and personal decisions on your behalf if you become unable to make your own decisions.			
Advance care/health directives	It is a legal document in which a person specifies what actions should be taken for their health if they are no longer able to make decisions for themselves due to illness or incapacity.			
Death benefit nominations for your super and life insurance in your super	There are several different types of beneficiary nominations that you may be able to enact: **A non-binding death benefit nomination** is used only as a guide by the super trustee when deciding who should receive your death benefit. Although the trustee can take your direction into account, they may choose to pay the benefit to another individual or to your estate. **A binding death benefit nomination** allows you to nominate who will receive your benefits in the event of your death, and it ensures that the super trustee is legally bound by your wishes. It is generally required to be renewed every three years. **A non-lapsing death benefit nomination** is a binding death benefit nomination that does not lapse. It will remain in force until such time as it is amended or revoked by you.			

As with other financial planning areas, estate planning must be reviewed regularly. 'Trigger events' that require review in an estate plan include:

- marriage, which automatically revokes a will; after you are married, you should make a new will
- separation, divorce or breakdowns in a relationship
- birth of an additional beneficiary
- death of a spouse, an existing beneficiary or other person nominated under the will to carry out a particular role, such as executor or trustee of a testamentary trust
- change in the personal or financial circumstances of nominated beneficiaries
- a material change in your financial circumstances
- a decline in health or some other variation of circumstances
- retirement

A few years afterwards, as Lisa battled with skin cancer, she shared some of her feelings with Mia at their meeting.

'My life will never be the same after cancer. People who haven't gone through this will never know what it is like to face the possibility of death. But I felt like I was the lucky one. I have you and my family to support me emotionally and financially. Not all of them are as lucky as me. Another patient I met during treatment had his cancer detected too late. His wife was eight months pregnant with their first child when he was diagnosed with melanoma. They did not have any trauma insurance, so they sold everything they had, including their cars and house, to pay for the expensive medication. After two years of continuous hospital appointments and distressing treatments, he passed away and left a significant financial struggle for his family. My results are clear, and now I only have regular checks with my doctor', Lisa said through tears. 'You once asked us questions based on the assumption that we could die in a few years or tomorrow. After I was diagnosed with cancer, the assumptions became a reality. I feel guilty for not appreciating the time I had. I now cherish every moment.'

She further added: 'I have a few concerns and I need your advice. When we first met, you recommended that we organise our estate planning. We followed your advice and set up wills and Enduring Powers of Attorney, although we did not think that we would need them so soon. I would like to review them and make some amendments this time'.

Lisa's brother, Nic, had died seven years ago in a car accident, leaving his wife Betty with their three children. A few years later, Betty remarried, but her new partner has a gambling addiction. Nic's youngest son, Tommy, has a disability and Lisa would like to make provisions for Tommy in her will. Lisa's younger son, Jason, wants to be a professional surfer and have a business providing surfing equipment one day. Lisa's older son, Alex, has been in a relationship with a single mum, Jane, and they had just moved into together.

Lisa told the adviser, 'I want to make a gift in my will to the Skin and Cancer Foundation. I want to contribute to the promotion of skin health in the community and I want to help those patients who need clinical treatment, but who cannot afford it themselves'.

'It is wonderful to help those who have a need. You need to update your will. We need to work with your solicitor to address these needs. A testamentary trust is one of the options for your situation', Mia said. 'It is a trust created by a will and it can provide assets protection for your children and financial support for Tommy.'

There are different types of testamentary trusts, including discretionary trusts and special disability trusts. The main benefits of testamentary trusts are their ability to protect assets and to reduce the tax liability for beneficiaries from income that is earned from the inheritance.

A testamentary trust provides asset protection for the beneficiaries of your estate who may face certain legal claims on their assets, divorce or bankruptcy. Because the assets in the testamentary trust do not belong to the beneficiaries, the trustee exercises their discretion to pay an income or asset entitlement to a beneficiary. As such, they are not subject to the risks that are associated with the beneficiaries who have high-risk occupations and potential relationship breakdowns. It also provides ongoing protection for vulnerable beneficiaries, and Richard and Lisa decide who will manage the testamentary trust on behalf of Tommy.

If a beneficiary takes their inheritance in their own name, they will pay tax at their personal marginal tax rate. There may be significant tax advantages with the testamentary trust if the beneficiary has:

- a high personal marginal tax rate
- a partner on a lower income
- minor children and grandchildren, or children and grandchildren with no or low taxable income.

A testamentary trust allows the person who controls it to split the income from the trust between family members such as a low-income partner or minor children. Children who receive income from a testamentary trust are taxed at adult tax rates (up to 45% excluding medicare levy) instead of minor penalty rates (up to 66%).

A testamentary trust is a great tool for wealth transfer, protection, and preservation in financial planning. Obtaining financial advice from the very beginning, and setting up properly, are key to ensuring your beneficiaries will maximise the benefit of this type of trust.

ESTATE AND NON-ESTATE ASSETS

Approximately one in five Australian families are 'blended', meaning that one or both of the partners were previously married, or that they have children from a previous relationship. In these cases, any estate planning will become more complex and sensitive.

When Lisa's friend Anna and her husband Michael came to see Mia, Anna had some concerns: 'Michael has two adult children from his previous marriage. His ex-wife is a real estate agent in Sydney. She is such a drama queen and you will never be able to predict what she will do next. That is one of the reasons we moved to Queensland. If something happened to Michael, I want to make sure that my rights will be protected, especially for the assets that we built up together after we were married'.

'Do you have a current will?' Mia had asked.

'We had them done when we were married, but we need to update them. I have heard that wills can be challenged', Anna mentioned.

'Yes, they can be challenged, but non-estate assets, for example, the assets under your joint names—your family home and your investment properties—are unlikely to be challenged. They are passed to the surviving partner automatically if one of you dies', Mia explained.

You may have heard the saying: 'where there's a will, there's a way'. It is usually used to encourage people to pursue their goals. But it also reflects the way people feel about estate planning. They think if you have a will, you will ensure your wealth is passed correctly to your loved ones. But it is not necessarily the case, as some assets never form part of an estate. Before you make a will, it is crucial that you understand the assets that you can give away by will, and those that you cannot.

Estate Assets

Individual assets are those that have your name only on the title. Common estate assets include bank accounts, real estate, investment accounts, shares, cars and business interests. Assets that are owned with someone else as tenants in common are also considered estate assets.

Non-Estate Assets

Non-estate assets will be passed to your heirs directly after you die. They generally include:

- assets under joint names
- assets held in a discretionary family trust or private company, in which you have an interest
- superannuation
- reversionary pensions or annuities
- life insurance policies.

Estate assets will pass under the terms of your will, but non-estate assets pass to your heirs under numerous other agreements and arrangements. Therefore, many of these situations require special attention. A solid estate plan will structure all your assets so that they are distributed according to your wishes—the plan includes much more than just the creation of wills.

Estate planning helps establish peace of mind in terms of managing the future of your family wealth and passing your life savings and assets to your loved ones. It can be a challenging and complex area, and a financial adviser must work with solicitors and accountants to help you plan for your 'final' intentions. For many people, 'how' you leave your legacy to your heirs is just as important as 'what' is passed onto them. The estate plan and legacy that you leave must reflect your core values, as you will never have a second chance to make a last impression.

Chapter 10

ADVICE PROCESS AND VALUE OF ADVICE

The financial advice industry has faced many challenges in the past decade, and there have been some great advisers who have made a real difference in lives of their clients. Understanding the financial planning process and the value of advice will help people who are seeking or receiving advice set suitable expectations.

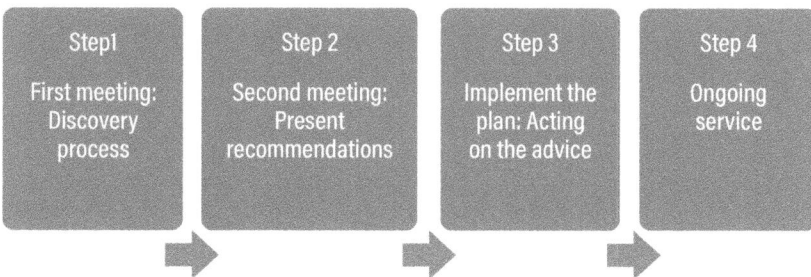

Step1	Step 2	Step 3	Step 4
First meeting: Discovery process	Second meeting: Present recommendations	Implement the plan: Acting on the advice	Ongoing service

Figure 14. The Financial Planning Process

THE FINANCIAL PLANNING PROCESS: FIRST MEETING

Planning for the future is hard work—but a trusted adviser can lighten the load considerably. The first meeting between a financial adviser and a prospective client is the starting point for your financial planning journey. It involves that crucial moment in which both adviser and client gauge whether they are the right fit for each other.

People will always feel a certain amount of angst when they meet their financial advisers for the first time—they do not know what to expect in terms of the outcomes of the meeting, what they will be asked to commit to or how much it will cost them.

To get the most from your first meeting, you should collect all your relevant financial information and bring it with you.

1. GATHERING INFORMATION

- **Collect recent statements for all investment accounts**—include the following
  - investment properties
  - term deposits and cash in the bank
  - superannuation
  - managed funds
  - direct shares
  - insurance bonds.
- **List your assets**—include the following
  - your home
  - other properties

  - motor vehicles
  - home contents
  - business assets (if you have some).
- **Create a debt profile, including the amounts that you owe and interest rates**
  - home mortgage
  - investment loans (property and others)
  - personal loans or car loans
  - credit cards.
- **Outline your income and expenses**
- **Collect your estate planning information**
  - your will
  - power of attorney
  - death benefit nominations for your super.
- **Identify your financial weaknesses**
  - Check your bank and credit card statements for the past few months and identify which purchases you have spent the most on and which have left you financially short.

2. SETTING FINANCIAL GOALS

- Create a list of financial priorities and involve your spouse (if applicable).

3. PREPARE A LIST OF QUESTIONS

- An honest professional will take the time to answer your questions so that you can make the best decision with your money. You can prepare a list of questions for your first meeting, on topics such as the following

- the services they provide
- their investing philosophy
- how they will communicate with you
- how they will measure and evaluate the performance of your investments
- how they will be paid.

At the first meeting, the adviser should take his or her time to understand the client's needs and goals. When Richard and Lisa came to see Mia, she asked numerous questions about their values, histories and concerns, alongside asking about their financial goals, dreams and aspirations. It may take more than one meeting to fully discuss your advice needs. In most cases, your first meeting with a financial adviser may be free. During this meeting, it is likely that your adviser will explain how they charge for their services and offer you an estimate for the cost of advice.

If you choose to proceed, your adviser should prepare a statement of advice (SOA), which is a document that formally outlines the recommendations that he or she has made. It also explains why these recommendations have been made and provides information regarding all the costs that are associated with the advice, as well as any payments or benefits that the adviser or licensee will receive. By the end of the first meeting, you should have a clear understanding of everything that was discussed—including the next steps that you should take.

After the first meeting, Mia developed appropriate recommendations based on the advice that Richard and Lisa were seeking, as well as on their circumstances. She then prepared advice documents, such as the SOA.

If you are the 'CEO' of your household, then consulting a financial adviser is like working with your CFO—as people tend to work with their financial advisers for many years. So, you should treat your first meeting like it is an interview for a new position in your team. There are some criteria that you can use to help you choose your financial adviser:

- **A licence to provide financial advice**—You should always look for a financial adviser who works for a firm holding an AFS licence issued by ASIC. You can verify that the financial planner is licenced by checking ASIC's MoneySmart website.
- **Education and experience**—Not all financial advisers have the same level of training or offer you the same depth of services. As such, in your search for an adviser, do your own diligence and ensure that your financial adviser is properly qualified and trained to meet your financial planning needs. Someone who holds a degree in financial planning or who is a certified financial planner is highly recommended.
- **The kinds of questions your financial adviser asks**—Did the adviser ask more about your money or about your life, values and goals? Those who only inquire about your money are only interested in your assets. For holistic financial planning, an adviser will ask a lot of questions about your life as it relates to money, then he or she will help you find the best solutions that align with your core values. If they do not have a clear understanding of

where you have been, who you are and where you want to go, they cannot do the right thing for you.

- **The adviser's listening skills**—Good advisers ask the right questions and do more listening than talking, as it gives them a window into their client's needs. If you feel that you are not communicating with a good listener, and that the adviser dominates the conversation, then you should move on. You should not expect someone who does not understand your problems to solve them. A good adviser needs to listen not only to the content of the message, but to the intent of it as well. Effective listening is anchored on understanding the message behind the message.

- **Language**—An important competency that advisers should have is the ability to make complicated matters seem understandable and straightforward. A good adviser will also be an excellent teacher who helps you increase your financial knowledge. Most clients are not financial experts, nor do they aim to be one. In the simplest terms, clients want to know what time it is, not how to build a clock. Great advisers don't force their feelings and opinions on clients and they try to encourage their clients to take action for their own reasons, even when they feel what their client wishes to do is opposed to what the adviser might perceive the client should be doing.

- **Investment philosophy**—One size doesn't fit all. Clients' investment strategies should fit in with their needs. A financial adviser is the one who can help you stay on track with your long-term goals, regardless of any short-term distractions. If the financial adviser does not have a clear investment philosophy to guide you through the journey, then he or she is likely someone who just wants to follow the crowd. Advisers who only sell whatever they are told to sell are not the people who you should look for.

In general, you should not expect to make immediate decisions when you first meet with a financial adviser. You have some learning to do first. If you walk out of an interview satisfied that the required bases have been or could be covered, then you will feel like you are partnering with a trustworthy professional. You know that you need someone to help you, so you need to feel that you have found one too.

AFTER THE FIRST MEETING

You can expect the second (and sometimes third) meeting to be more tactical. Financial advisers will recommend strategies and products in the form of advice documents—the SOA—which help you achieve your goals. You will then have a stronger understanding of where you are now, where you want to be and how you will get there. The cost of preparing the SOA will be billed to you, or perhaps deducted with your permission from the balance of your investment.

Mia and her administration team established the plan that Richard and Lisa agreed to after the second meeting and ensured that everything was completed correctly. If you decide to accept the adviser's recommendations, there might be a fee to cover the administration work involved with implementing the advice. The amount charged should reflect the complexity of the recommendations and the amount of work that is required. It may take up to a few months from the first meeting for your financial plan to be implemented.

After 12 months of engaging in their financial planning process, Richard and Lisa had their first review meeting with Mia. Depending on the life stage you are in and the complexity of your financial plan, you may decide to have review meetings annually, half-yearly or more often. If you have agreed to receive ongoing advice, then you must understand what your ongoing advice fee covers. Services may include:

- regular reviews with your financial adviser
- regular reports on your investment portfolio
- phone or email access to your adviser or an associate
- newsletters and seminar invitations.

The adviser may offer different levels of ongoing service that will determine the ongoing cost and the amount of contact that you can have with him or her. How your adviser charges fees depends on your needs and the adviser's business model. Some advisers may charge one fee for all of their services, while others may charge more than three types of fees.

VALUE OF ADVICE

The value of advice differs from person to person at different stages of their lives. It is difficult to understand and appreciate the value of advice unless you experience it first-hand, as the value of advice extends beyond financial benefits. The emotional and behavioural aspects of advice are equally important.

Financial Benefits

Good advice leads to better financial decision-making. The financial benefits of receiving advice may be quantified by comparing the results of situations in which you had or did not have advice. These benefits can include more income in retirement, lower tax bills and demonstrably enhanced net wealth and protection from unexpected life events.

Emotional Benefits

The significant emotional benefits of receiving advice include peace of mind and greater confidence in managing finances. Life is dynamic and unpredictable—marriage, children, divorce, unemployment, promotions and inheritance are all elements of your life that can affect your financial wellbeing. Knowing that another person is helping you stay on top of your financial matters and that they are available during a crisis is more than a comfort.

Behavioural Benefits

Financial advice addresses longer-term structural habits. It trains better behaviour, and advised clients have better control of their finances. They save and invest more and are better prepared to manage life's unexpected events. There is significant research showing that the return that average investors receive is significantly lower than that of the market. This is because of their behaviour—their lack of investment discipline. One important reason to use a financial adviser is that you want to reduce the risk of investing.

WHEN IS THE BEST TIME TO SEE AN ADVISER?

The biggest obstacle in the way of our financial success is a delay. Many people seek advice only when they think they need it. Major life-changing events like starting a new business, buying a house, inheriting money, a pending divorce or retiring, can all provoke people to consider using an adviser. They are more likely to pay for the cure for problems instead of investing in prevention.

If you wait for the perfect time to start your financial plan, that day may never come along. The best way to arrive early at your financial destination is to start early, so you can benefit from good money management habits and compound interest from early investments.

FINANCIAL PLANNING IN AUSTRALIA

Financial planning had not emerged as a distinct field until the 1970s, so most Australians in need of financial advice depended on their bankers, accountants and insurance agents at that time. However, in the proceeding couple of decades, not only did financial planning become established as a distinct discipline, the demand for financial advice also grew significantly, which led to the introduction of an entirely new class of financial advisers.

The widely recognised importance of the financial planning industry and the rapid growth it has experienced in the last few decades has naturally resulted in the industry receiving increased attention from regulators. The Federal Government implemented the Future of Financial Advice (FOFA) reforms in July 2013, which aimed to ensure the industry's professional integrity and transparency. Additionally, the Royal Commission into Misconduct in the Banking, Superannuation and Financial Services Industry has placed significant regulatory pressure on industry operators.

Although there are many highly qualified, ethical and client-focused advisers, there have been several cases of poor financial advice from industry professionals that have led to significant losses for clients. The changes that we experienced in the last few years address these concerns, as discussed below.

Commissions

Commissions and volume-based payments for recommending financial products can influence the advice that financial advisers offer, which is the area in which conflicts of interest arise the most. Changes to the commission structure for financial products include the following:

- Commissions on new investments and super products were banned as at 1 July 2013.

- Advisers can receive ongoing commissions from financial products that were bought before 1 July 2013, which we called 'grandfathered commissions'. The Australian government introduced legislation that banned grandfathered commissions from 1 Jan 2021.
- Many advisers still receive commissions on life insurance products. The Australian government capped life insurance commissions that financial advisers would receive in 2017—and the cap may reduce even more in the future.

Professional and Educational Standards

Professional and Educational Standards Legislation came into effect on 1 January 2019, imposing restrictions in terms of who can be called a 'financial planner' and 'financial adviser'. New financial advisers or planners are required to hold a relevant bachelor or higher degree before commencing work, pass an exam, and complete a year of work and training. Experienced financial advisers must have passed an exam by 1 October 2022, and reach an educational standard that is equivalent to an approved degree by 1 January 2026. All financial advisers must meet continuing professional development requirements.

Disclosure of Advice Fees

If clients have agreed to ongoing advice, they will receive an annual fee disclosure statement from their adviser that outlines the fees that the adviser was paid, the services that were provided by the adviser, and the services that the clients were entitled to receive within the previous 12 months. Clients can end their ongoing relationships with their advisers at any time by notifying them in writing.

Best Interest Obligations

Best interest obligations under the Corporations Act require advisers to act in the best interests of their clients when providing personal advice. The ongoing effects of the Future of Financial Advice laws and the royal commission's findings have promoted a level of financial service in which advice is delivered in a way that clearly and demonstrably strives for the clients' best interests.

Regulatory changes and heightened professional standards mitigate conflicts of interest, as well as fees for no advice, and help ensure that consumers receive better quality advice. However, the costs of advice has increased accordingly in the last few years. There are some alternatives for clients who have simple needs and a limited capacity to pay:

- **Phone-based advice**—This service is often used for single-issue advice that can be handled over the phone, in conjunction with a follow-up email or letter.
- **Robo-advice**—This involves financial advice that is delivered by a computer instead of a human financial adviser. It may be more suitable for simple issues, such as choosing appropriate investments.

How Robo-Advice Works

You would need to register with a digital advice website and log in to answer questions relating to your income and expenses, assets and liabilities, goals, objectives and risk tolerance. This provides your robo-adviser with information about your financial situation and goals. The website's algorithm then considers this information before making recommendations. Robo-advice produces an automated SOA that explains the recommendations made and other relevant information. Robo-advisers may have lower advice fees than traditional financial advisers, as they are not using people to assess clients' needs. However, unlike a person, a computer cannot clarify your goals or dreams, discuss any issues with you or make adjustments if your financial life is not progressing as planned.

* * *

The future of the Australian financial advice industry is being reshaped in real-time—the effects of which create both a confronting environment and significant opportunities for advisers. Advisers who adapt and evolve the nature of their methods and how they are conducted will find themselves in a stronger position—one in which they are trusted, respected and valued by the community as professionals offering a valuable service. Working with an adviser who is knowledgeable in the broad discipline of financial planning and who completely focuses on your life is crucial for your financial wellbeing.

Chapter 11

PLANNING TO LIVE
THE DREAM

Based on a survey of 2,635 Australians aged between 23 and 71, the FPA's (2017) 'Live the Dream' national research report stated that 'almost one in four Australians (23%) believe they are definitely or mostly living the dream'.

Australians believe that 'living the dream' signifies having the lifestyle of their choice. They also strongly emphasise the importance of having financial freedom and independence, creating safety and security for their family and owning a home.

Figure 15 represents survey responses to the question: *What does the phrase 'living the dream' mean to you?*

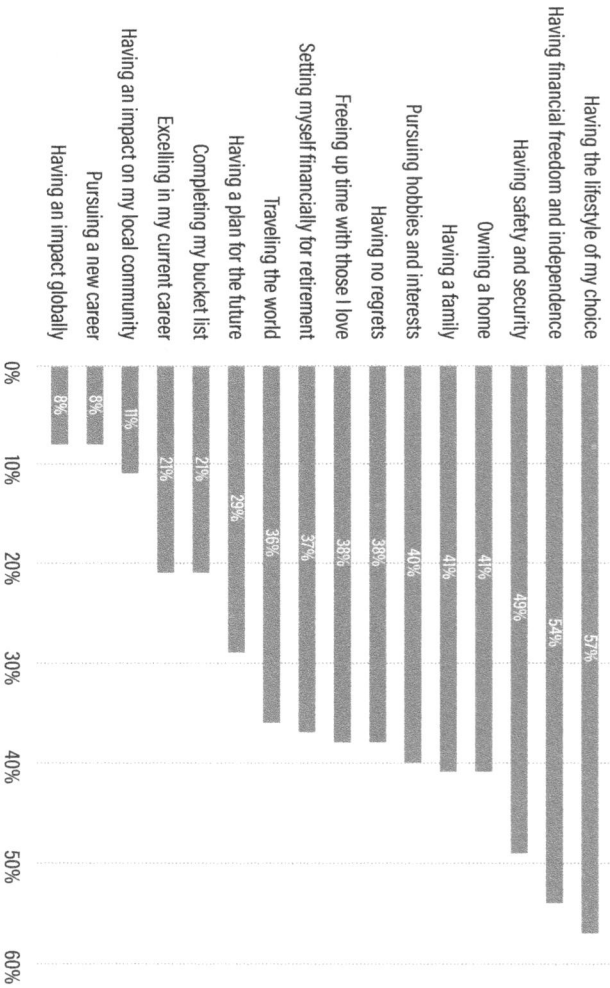

Figure 15. 'Living the Dream' Components

Source: FPA (2017)

Having the lifestyle of my choice — 57%
Having financial freedom and independence — 54%
Having safety and security — 49%
Owning a home — 41%
Having a family — 41%
Pursuing hobbies and interests — 40%
Having no regrets — 38%
Freeing up time with those I love — 38%
Setting myself financially for retirement — 37%
Travelling the world — 36%
Having a plan for the future — 29%
Completing my bucket list — 21%
Excelling in my current career — 21%
Having an impact on my local community — 11%
Pursuing a new career — 8%
Having an impact globally — 8%

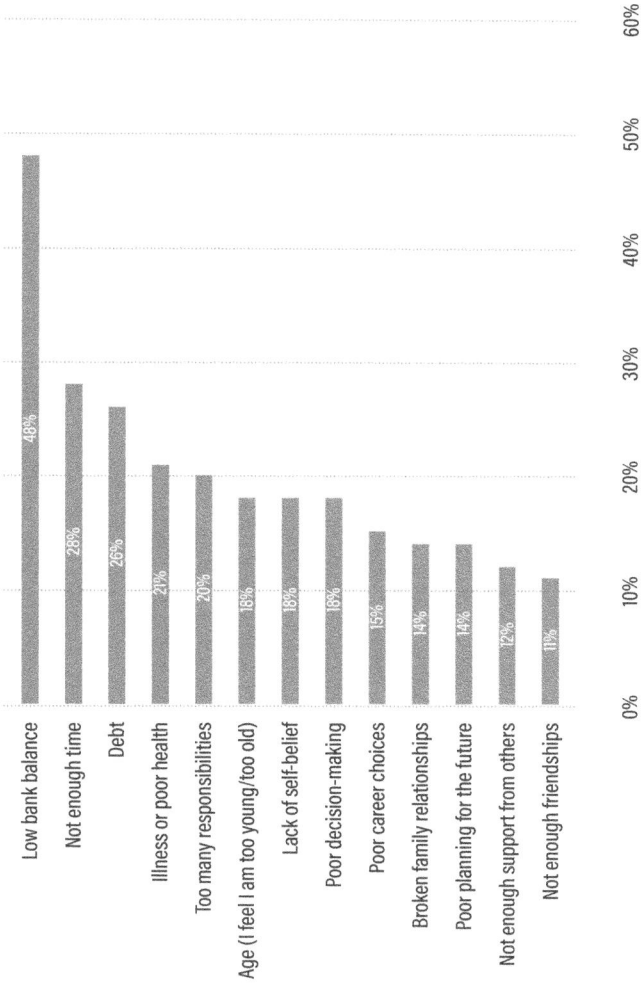

Figure 16. 'Living the Dream' Inhibitors

Source: FPA (2017)

Finance is the most significant block to living the dream—in fact, two of the three most significant factors that prevent us from living our dreams are financial in nature. Having a low bank balance appears to be the biggest blocker, while debt also appears as another similarly significant obstacle.

Figure 16 represents survey responses to the question: *What do you believe is preventing you from 'living the dream'?*

Whether we like it or not, there is a price tag attached to almost everything that we want in life. Living your dream is no exception. Based on the survey, Australians who are living the dream are nearly twice as likely to seek advice from a financial adviser (66 per cent) than those who are not living the dream (38 per cent).

According to the survey, almost 73 per cent of Australians find planning their lives difficult, and the most difficult parts include:

- not knowing what they want (36 per cent)
- finding the right resources to help create a plan (32 per cent)
- finding the time to map out a plan (29 per cent)
- sticking to a plan if they make one (23 per cent).

FINANCIAL WELLBEING & FINANCIAL FREEDOM

Financial wellbeing is a different thing to being wealthy. Wealth is typically measured by the total value of your financial assets less any financial debts. The reality is that you can simultaneously have high net wealth and lack financial wellbeing, depending on how you manage your money.

Financial wellbeing entails having the financial security to enjoy your life, without worrying about money. It includes:

- being able to keep up with debt repayments, living costs and other financial obligations
- having enough emergency funds to handle any unexpected expenses
- being free from financial stress
- feeling secure and in control of your finances now, in the future, and when life takes an unexpected turn

Many Australians enjoy comparatively high wealth, according to global standards, but the average level of financial wellbeing for Australians is low. Australians have low levels of financial confidence and literacy, and any disastrous life events (e.g. pandemic, divorce, ill health, unemployment or losing a partner) can quickly derail their lives.

Based on the 2019 Household Financial Comfort Report from ME Bank, one in four Australians are living from pay to pay, without even having $1,000 in their accounts for emergencies. Many of us learned a hard lesson during the global pandemic after we witnessed how quickly jobs can disappear and businesses can shut down. Planning our own financial future became more important than ever.

Financial freedom means different things to different people, but for everyone it means a higher level of financial wellbeing. Financial freedom means making the most of your life without relying on pay cheques because passive income from your money-making machine covers all your expenses.

Building a money-making machine is the key to your financial success and it doesn't happen overnight. The more assets you accumulate in your money-making machine, the less you rely on your paying job, and it helps you take one step closer to your goals.

STEPS FOR CREATING FINANCIAL FREEDOM AND LIVING THE DREAM

'Some people die at 25 and aren't buried until 75', Benjamin Franklin once famously stated. What he meant is that many people never truly live. They merely exist, without a purposeful design. The truth is, we all love to dream. When we are young, we are full of energy—every new day holds a discovery, and we want to experience and learn as much as possible. We feel like we could change the world—we feel alive.

Soon after they start growing older, some seem to stop dreaming as well. Everything becomes a routine and they become tied up with their current situation, which keeps them from living their ideal life. It is not necessarily what they want, but it is something safe and familiar (see Figure 17).

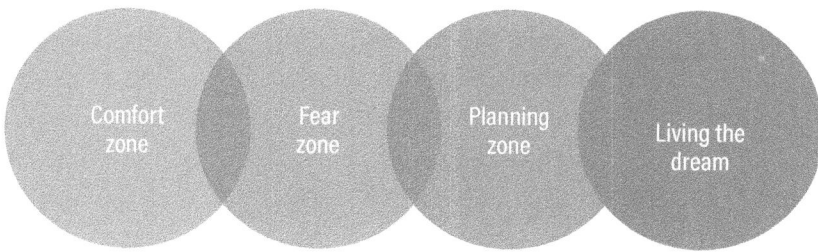

Figure 17. The Different Zones of 'Living the Dream'

THE COMFORT ZONE

It seems that when it comes to money, the only skills that most people have are working hard and paying the bills. They go to work, earn an income and spend or save (ideally), then take out debts for the big purchases such as buying a house. It seems like they are just waking up every day to go to work and pay the bills. It may even feel strange when they find themselves with some money in their pockets, since they are so used to not having enough.

You may aspire to have more money in the bank and less tied up in a mortgage. You may dream of building wealth by investing in the share market and buying investment properties, or you may want to start your own business. However, if you stay in your comfort zone and rarely make decisions that require a sacrifice or some risk, these aspirations may not materialise.

THE FEAR ZONE

Soon after you decide to leave the comfort zone, you may feel the discomfort of insecurity and the fear of unforeseen changes (for which you do not feel prepared). You may experience both a fear of not having enough money and a fear of trying something new. You are now in the fear zone.

When we encounter new opportunities, we feel both delighted and fearful—we may fear putting our trust in the wrong person for guidance, or fear being told we need to change and sacrifice, or give up what we are enjoying now. Our fear of stepping into the unknown can prompt us to set aside our dreams.

You can become stuck in a loop, repeating the same patterns, and you may believe that you have no control over anything in your life. This can dilute your energy and pressure you, leading you to experience more lows than highs in your life. As time passes, you may feel a growing sense of regret.

THE PLANNING ZONE

A dream written down with a date becomes a **goal.** *A goal broken down into steps becomes a* **plan.** *A plan backed by* **action** *makes your dreams* **come true.**

–Greg Reid, author of *Wealth Made Easy*

When your desire to fulfil your dreams is more prominent than your fear of change, you start to plan—you plan to turn your dreams into reality. There are definite steps you can take to create ongoing financial wellbeing and freedom so you can achieve those dreams, with the help of a trusted adviser:

- Understand where you have been and where you are now financially.

- Discover what you want in your life.
- Set aside enough emergency funds for unexpected events.
- Organise sufficient insurance cover for more significant disasters (e.g. disability, illness and death).
- Establish a debt management strategy to immediately pay off your bad debts and effectively manage your good debts.
- Focus on actively growing your wealth by creating a money-making machine.
- Create a retirement plan and start implementing it early.
- Have an estate plan in place.

Many of us find that money is a difficult topic to talk about. Having open and transparent conversations about money with the people around us helps us make better financial decisions. Discussing your financial options with not only your financial adviser, but also your family, can help you avoid mistakes and offer you the guidance and support that you need.

Creating a money-making machine and working towards your financial freedom with your loved ones are the most important steps you can take to start living the life of your dreams.

LIVE THE DREAM

Ask yourself: *How do I live my life now? Do I live by design or by default?*

Living by design signifies that you are the creator of your life. Conversely, living by default means that you are just reacting to whatever you encounter in your life and that you are making no conscious or deliberate action towards having the life you want.

You may have a dream and a plan, and you may be taking some action towards it, but you will not achieve anything significant if your effort is not consistent. Success is not the moment when you realise your goal. Every time you consciously take action to achieve your dream is a moment of success. You set goals, conquer your objectives and then set new goals—and then you eventually find your purpose and live the life of your dreams.

* * *

It has been 17 years since Richard and Lisa created their first financial plan with Mia. They went to Mia's office and had their review meeting.

'Congratulations!' Mia said, with a big smile on her face. 'You've achieved your biggest goal. You can retire anytime you choose now because you've achieved your financial freedom. Your investments—both super and non-super—now generate enough income for you to live comfortably without working. You achieved your goals three years earlier than planned. When would you like to retire, Richard?'

'I don't want to retire now!' Richard unexpectedly revealed, causing Lisa and Mia to burst into laughter. 'What am I supposed to do if I retire at age 55? I want to work as long as I can. Well,

I mean, I wanted to be in the financial position to have the option', he added.

'How do you feel now, knowing that you achieved your goals and are in the position to retire anytime?' Mia asked.

'Great', he answered simply. 'Having money and being able to choose what to do makes it a lot easier to enjoy life. I finally feel like I am in the driver's seat and that I'm driving my own destiny.'

When Mia asked Lisa the same question, Lisa answered: 'I achieved my biggest dream a few years ago. I have my successful life-coaching business and I help people create success, love and happiness in their lives. My children are grown up now, so they don't need me around anymore. I am going to finish my Master of Psychology this year and want to help even more people'.

'Do you have any new dreams that you want to achieve?' Mia asked the couple.

'I started doing photography five years ago and I invested a bit of money on camera gear. I would like to have my own exhibition in the next three years', Richard answered.

'A bit of money?' Lisa repeated, smiling. 'It's a lot! But those photos capture memorable moments and events of our lives.'

'That's what it's all about. You can spend your time on the things that you love the most now', Mia enthused.

The truth is that if you want to have the best life with the money you have, you do not need to be a millionaire; you just need to work with someone who really understands money, and be smart with how you manage your money. If you diligently create a framework—one that is based on real and solid financial planning—then, through it, you can build the life you want. In essence, having your best life signifies that you are happy with who you are, satisfied with what you have and fulfilled by what you do.

This will be a life well lived!

Epilogue

WHY DID I WRITE THIS BOOK?

As a financial adviser, I work every day with people and money BUT money is just one of the elements of a fulfilling and happy life. The purpose of this book is to show you how to maximise the benefits of your money to design, create and live your best life.

However, the recent changes in the embattled financial services industry have created both confusion for consumers and uncertainty for advisers.

Consumers are asking: What do financial advisers actually do? How can I achieve my goals with the help of a trusted adviser? They need answers.

When it comes to accessing trusted financial advice, the majority of Australians fall into one of these three categories:

- those who maintain an ongoing relationship with a financial adviser
- those who have one-off experiences with a financial adviser
- those who have never seen a financial adviser.

Those who have worked with a financial adviser may have received their financial plans in written form as a Statement of Advice (SOA). For most, this document is far too complex to understand. Even the fine print on the back of the SOA generally doesn't help clients' understanding, as not many can read them thoroughly. It is an adviser's job to explain complex financial planning concepts as simply as possible—not just assume it makes sense.

Most people who have a one-off experience with an adviser don't maintain an ongoing relationship because of affordability, and because they can't see the real value of the advice.

People who have never seen an adviser have various reasons: they often don't know where to start with the whole process; they may not trust financial advisers; or they may consider financial advice to be too expensive. Some of them are too afraid to reach out to a financial adviser for fear of not having enough, not knowing enough, or being told their dreams just aren't achievable.

When advisers provide advice, our clients' risk management strategies, investment portfolio and cash flow modelling are important. But these are inputs, not outputs. In our clients' eyes, what are important are peace of mind, a sense of wellbeing and freedom to pursue the life they want.

The characters in this book are fictional, but their questions and concerns are real. They represent the real lives and scenarios I have advised over the last decade.

WHAT DRIVES ME?

As financial advisers, I believe that before we help our clients to figure out what they want out of life, we need to ask ourselves that same question. Our life journey is similar to that of the clients we serve. We have our desires and ambitions for success, and fears and frustrations from life's challenges.

A few years ago, I asked myself the 'Three George Kinder Questions' (see page 46) and began planning and designing my life based on my responses. I believe financial advisers who focus on building their own lives will serve others' lives better. Advisers who create a balanced life for themselves will create a business that is rewarding and successful. If you want to help others fulfil their dreams, your first step is to do that for yourself.

My greatest satisfaction as an adviser comes from helping my clients enjoy their journey, not just their destination, by working with them as they plan the life they want, not just the placement of their money. I want them to look back on their lives after 20 or 30 years, and enjoy the pleasure that comes from a well-travelled journey.

And I want that for me too.

After all, a life lived well every day is both the journey and the destination.

Helen Nan

CFP®, ADFS (FP), DFS, B.Art, MBA, MAcc

Invitation

Contact Helen to arrange a no-obligation call or subscribe to her newsletter as a positive step towards a better financial future. Go to her website at www.compoundfreedom.au

Contact: (07) 3289 6745
Email: helen.nan@wlplanning.com.au
PO BOX 3007 Sunnybank South QLD 4109

Reference List

Chapter 1

Eker, T Harv 2005, *Secret of the millionaire mind: mastering the inner game of wealth*, HarperCollins Publishers, New York.

Investopedia 2019, *What is your money personality type*, Investopedia, viewed 15 May 2019. <https://www.investopedia.com/articles/basics/07/money-personality.asp>

Stewart, E & Hinchliffe, J 2018, *Why discovering your money personality could help fix your money problems*, ABC News, viewed 15 May 2019, <https://www.abc.net.au/news/2018-02-08/what-is-your-money-personality-type/9348666>

Chapter 2

Kinder, G 2000, *Seven stages of money maturity*, Dell Publishing, Canada.

Klontz, B 2014, *Psychology of wealth: Psychological factors associated with high income*, Journal of Financial Planning, viewed 7 June 2019, <https://www.yourmentalwealthadvisors.com/sites/default/files/users/nathanwalsh3/Studies/studytwo/The%20Psychology%20of%20Wealth%20-%20Psychological%20Factors%20Associated%20with%20High%20Income%20-%20Journal%20of%20Financial%20Planning%20-%202014.pdf>

Vohwinkle, J 2019, *Make a personal budget in 6 steps*, the balance, viewed 24 March 2019, <https://www.thebalance.com/how-to-make-a-budget-1289587>

Chapter 3

Abraham, K 2017, *Focus*, Passion Press, Australia.

Bachrach, B 1996, *Value based selling*, Aim High Publishing, America.

Kinder, G & Glavan, S 2006, *Lighting the torch*, FPA Press, America.

Chapter 4

Kaplan Professional 2018, *Field underwriting engagement and skills: Part 1*, Kaplan Professional, viewed 5 August 2019, <https://ontrack.mykaplan.edu.au/1801-field-underwriting-engagement-and-skills-part-1/2/>

Martin, F & Connell, E 2017, *Cancer in Australia*, Australian Institute of Health and Welfare, viewed 15 May 2019, <https://www.aihw.gov.au/getmedia/54fec0ca-4404-4f45-8fc3-4490056681a7/20545.pdf.aspx?inline=true>

Unwin, C 2015, *The risk workshop: How to turn a grudge purchase into a fantastic opportunity*, Australia.

Warner, R 2018, *Life insurance adequacy*, Ricewarner, viewed 3 July 2019, <https://www.ricewarner.com/life-insurance-adequacy/>

Chapter 5

ASIC's Moneysmart 2023, *Cryptocurrencies*, ASIC Moneysmart, viewed 5 January 2023, <https://moneysmart.gov.au/investment-warnings/cryptocurrencies>

FinaMetrica 2019, *What is risk tolerance*, Finametrica, viewed 30 October 2019, <https://www.riskprofiling.com/How-it-Works>

Investopedia, *How to invest in cryptocurrency*, Investopedia, viewed 3 January 2023, <https://www.investopedia.com/investing-in-cryptocurrency-5215269#:~:text=Cryptocurrency%20is%20digital%20money%20that,or%20through%20certain%20broker%2Ddealers.>

Kinder, G 2000, *Seven stages of money maturity*, Dell Publishing, Canada.

Koulizos, P & Zacharia, Z 2013, *Property Vs Shares*, Wrightbooks, Australia.

MLC 2019, *Investment concepts – Dollar cost averaging*, MLC, viewed 18 May 2019, <https://www.mlc.com.au/content/dam/mlc/documents/pdf/advice/Dollar-cost-averaging.pdf>

Robbins, T & Mallouk, P 2018, *Unshakeable*, Simon & Schuster, UK.

Vanguard 2019, *2019 Vanguard index chart*, Vanguard, viewed 21 October 2019, <https://static.vgcontent.info/crp/intl/auw/docs/resources/2019_index_chart.pdf?20200221|163928>

West, S, Saylor, D & Anthony, M 2012, *The financial professional's storybook,* Adviser Insights Press, America.

Chapter 6

ACCC 2023, *Scams robbed Australians of more than $2 billion last year,* viewed 29 January 2023, <https://www.accc.gov.au/media-release/scams-robbed-australians-of-more-than-2-billion-last-year#:~:text=Reported%20losses%20to%20all%20organisations,were%20well%20over%20%242%20billion.>

ASIC's Moneysmart 2019, *Borrowing to invest,* viewed 11 August 2019, <https://www.moneysmart.gov.au/investing/borrowing-to-invest>

ASIC's Moneysmart 2017, *Margin lending,* viewed 11 August 2019, <https://www.moneysmart.gov.au/investing/borrowing-to-invest/margin-loans>

ASIC's Moneysmart 2019, *Investment scams,* viewed 12 August 2019, <https://moneysmart.gov.au/investment-warnings/investment-scams>

Kaplan Professional 2018, *Gearing 101*, Kaplan Professional, viewed 1 August 2019, <https://ontrack.mykaplan.edu.au/1808-gearing-101/2/>

Kaplan Professional 2018, *How the GFC shaped Australia's regulation of margin lending*, Kaplan Professional, viewed 2 August 2019, <https://ontrack.mykaplan.edu.au/1812-how-the-gfc-shaped-australias-regulation-of-margin-lending/2/>

Koulizos, P & Zacharia, Z 2013, *Property Vs Shares*, Wright-books, Australia.

MLC 2019, *Narrowing the retirement savings gap for women*, viewed 5 August 2019, <https://www.mlc.com.au/personal/retirement/retirement-today/narrowing-the-retirement-savings-gap-for-women>

Chapter 7

Anthony, M 2014, *The new retirementality*, John Wiley & Sons, Canada.

Anthony, M 2006, *Your clients for life*, Dearborn Trade Publishing, America.

Canstar 2019, *Highest term deposit rates: November 2019*, viewed 9 November 2019, <https://www.canstar.com.au/term-deposits/highest-term-deposit-rates/>

Kaplan Professional 2019, *Helping people into aged care*, Kaplan Professional, viewed 25 August 2019, <https://cdn.mykaplan.edu.au/201908-helping-people-into-aged-care/index.html#/>

Kaplan Professional 2017, *Retirement is different*, Kaplan Professional, viewed 3 July 2019, <https://ontrack.mykaplan.edu.au/1712-retirement-is-different/2/>

MGD Wealth 2019, *Sequencing risk*, MGD wealth, viewed 10 November 2019, <https://mgdwealth.com.au/wp-content/uploads/2018/09/Sequencing-Risk-Why-the-path-of-your-investmetn-returns-matters-when-you-retire.pdf>

MLC 2019, *Setting up for retirement success*, MLC, viewed 2 May 2019, <https://www.mlc.com.au/personal/retirement/retirement-today/setting-up-for-retirement-success>

MLC 2019, *How much can you afford to spend in retirement*, MLC, viewed 3 May 2019, <https://www.mlc.com.au/personal/retirement/retirement-today/how-much-can-you-afford-to-spend-in-retirement>

Myagedcare 2023, *Home care package costs and fees*, viewed 18 January 2023, <https://www.myagedcare.gov.au/home-care-package-costs-and-fees>

Myagedcare 2023, *Short-term care*, viewed 18 January 2023, <https://www.myagedcare.gov.au/short-term-care>

The Association of Superannuation Funds of Australia 2022, *ASFA Retirement standard*, viewed 3 January 2023, <https://www.superannuation.asn.au/ArticleDocuments/ArticleDocuments/269/2211-ASFA_Retirement_Standard_Budgets_September_2022_quarter.pdf.aspx?Embed=Y>

West, S, Saylor, D & Anthony, M 2012, *The financial professional's storybook*, Adviser Insights Press, America.

Chapter 8

Joelson, R 2019, *Managing difficult life transitions*, viewed 14 July 2019, <https://richardbjoelsondsw.com/articles/managing-difficult-life-transitions/>

Zurich 2019, *Bull v bear*, Zurich, viewed 19 Aug 2019, <https://www.zurich.com.au/advisers/news/investment-insights/2019/bulls-vs-bears.html>

Chapter 9

Australian Seniors 2019, *Understanding a Last Will & Testament in Layman's terms*, Australian Seniors, viewed 7 July 2019, <https://www.seniors.com.au/funeral-insurance/discover/understanding-last-will-testament>

The Australian 2016, *It's a battle of wills when estates are contested*, The Australian, viewed 5 May 2019, <https://www.theaustralian.com.au/nation/inquirer/its-a-battle-of-wills-when-estates-are-contested/news-story/87ccb8b42cb74f-683b5376ebf0fbb61c>

Chapter 10

AFP Business Brokers 2019, *What is the Australian Financial Planning Industry*, AFP Business Brokers, viewed 20 July 2019, <http://www.afpbb.com.au/Resources/TheFinancialPlanningIndustry.aspx>

ASIC's Moneysmart 2018, *Financial advice costs*, ASIC's Moneysmart, viewed 18 July 2019, <https://www.moneysmart.gov.au/investing/financial-advice/financial-advice-costs>

ASIC's Moneysmart 2018, *Type of financial advice*, ASIC's Moneysmart, viewed 19 July 2019, <https://www.moneysmart.gov.au/investing/financial-advice/types-of-financial-advice>

Association of Financial Adviser 2018, *Value of advice 2018*, AFA, viewed 5 July 2019, <https://www.afa.asn.au/sites/default/files/uploaded-content/field_f_content_file/afa_report_oct_2018_final.pdf>

Financial Planning Association of Australia 2019, *The future of financial planning*, viewed 4 November 2019, <https://fpa.com.au/news/the-future-of-financial-planning/>

Financial Planning Association of Australia 2019, *Royal Commission Wrap-up*, Financial Planning Association of Australia, viewed 1 July 2019, <https://fpa.com.au/wp-content/uploads/2019/03/FPA-Royal-Commission-Wrap-25-Feb.pdf>

Hogan, C 2019, *How to prepare for a meeting with a financial planner*, DaveRamsey, viewed 3 March 2019, <https://www.daveramsey.com/blog/how-to-prepare-meeting-financial-planner>

Chapter 11

Colonial First State 2019, *Taking charge of your financial wellbeing*, Colonial First State, viewed 14 September 2019, <https://www3.colonialfirststate.com.au/content/dam/colonial-first-state/docs/adviser/campaign/financial-wellbeing/C-5-26116-FS7212-FW-20190829.pdf>

Financial Planning Association of Australia 2017, *Live the dream*, FPA, viewed 23 June 2019, <http://www.moneyandlife.com.au/wp-content/uploads/2017/08/FPA-Live-the-Dream-2017-Research-Report-FINAL.pdf>

Bibliography

Diliberto, R 2006, *Financial planning – The next step*, FPA Press, America.

Evangelidis, J 2012, *What do financial planning clients really want*, Lawbook Co, Australia.

Kiyosaki, R & Lechter, S 2004, *Rich Dad Poor Dad*, TechPress, America.

MLC 2019, *Understanding series*, MLC, viewed 18 May 2019, <https://www.mlc.com.au/personal/understanding-series#/anchor_HVTGBRj4>

Murry, N 1996, *The excellent investment advisor*, Nick Murray, America.

Parisse, A & Richman, D 2006, *Questions great financial advisors ask - and investors need to know*, Kaplan Publishing, America.

West, S, Saylor, D & Anthony, M 2012, *The financial professional's storybook*, Adviser Insights Press, America.

West, S & Anthony, M 2000, *Storyselling for financial advisors*, Kaplan Publishing, America.

List of Figures

List of Tables

List of Abbreviations

AFS	Australian Financial Services
ASFA	Association of Super Funds of Australia
ASIC	Australian Securities and Investments Commission
ASX	Australian Securities Exchange
CGT	Capital gains tax
ETF	Exchange traded fund
FI	Fixed interest
GFC	Global financial crisis
GST	Goods and services tax
IP	Income protection
LVR	Loan to value ratio
RAD	Refundable accommodation deposit
SMA	Separately managed account
SMSF	Self-managed super fund
SOA	Statement of advice
TPD	Total and permanent disability

www.ingramcontent.com/pod-product-compliance
Lightning Source LLC
Chambersburg PA
CBHW040916210326
41597CB00030B/5102